Edward Gilpin Johnson

The Best Letters of Lord Chesterfield

Letters to his Son, and Letters to his Godson

Edward Gilpin Johnson

The Best Letters of Lord Chesterfield
Letters to his Son, and Letters to his Godson

ISBN/EAN: 9783744722018

Printed in Europe, USA, Canada, Australia, Japan

Cover: Foto ©ninafisch / pixelio.de

More available books at **www.hansebooks.com**

THE BEST LETTERS

OF

LORD CHESTERFIELD

Letters to his Son
AND
Letters to his Godson

By PHILIP DORMER STANHOPE
EARL OF CHESTERFIELD

𝔈𝔡𝔦𝔱𝔢𝔡 𝔴𝔦𝔱𝔥 𝔞𝔫 𝔍𝔫𝔱𝔯𝔬𝔡𝔲𝔠𝔱𝔦𝔬𝔫
By EDWARD GILPIN JOHNSON

CHICAGO
A. C. McCLURG AND COMPANY
1893

CONTENTS.

	PAGE
INTRODUCTION	9

Chesterfield's Letters to his Son.

LETTER
I. Good Breeding Relative and General 27
II. A Genteel Manner Important 30
III. True Praise. — Elementary Politeness 33
IV. Dancing. — All Things should be Done Well . . 36
V. Elocution : Method of Demosthenes 37
VI. Inattention. — Knowledge of Mankind 38
VII. Never Attack a Corps Collectively 41
VIII. On Travelling Intelligently 42
IX. True Pleasure Inconsistent with Vice 45
X. The " Absent Man." — Thoughtfulness 48
XI. A Showy Binding 50
XII. Epistolary Models 52
XIII. Tolerance and Truth Recommended 53
XIV. Caution in Forming Friendships 55
XV. The Art of Pleasing 59
XVI. On Combining Study with Pleasure 65
XVII. A Wise Guide the Best Friend 66
XVIII. The Value of Time 68
XIX. Time Well and Time Ill Spent 70
XX. Right Use of Learning 74
XXI. The Graces. — Absurdity of Laughter 77
XXII. Dissimulation found not only in Courts 81
XXIII. An Awkward Man at Court 83
XXIV. The Lazy Mind and the Frivolous Mind 85
XXV. How History should be read 89
XXVI. General Character of Women 90
XXVII. Our Tendency to exalt the Past 94
XXVIII. Against Refinements of Casuistry 96

Letter		Page
XXIX.	True Good Company Defined	98
XXX.	Conduct in Good Company	102
XXXI.	Rules for Conduct in Good Company	109
XXXII.	Importance of the Graces, etc.	115
XXXIII.	The Importance of Dress	120
XXXIV.	On Prejudices. — Liberty of the Press	123
XXXV.	Dignity of Manners Recommended	129
XXXVI.	Court Manners and Methods	131
XXXVII.	On Awkwardness and Absence of Mind	133
XXXVIII.	Vulgarisms. — An Awkward Man, etc.	139
XXXIX.	Three Sorts of Good Breeding	143
XL.	The same Subject continued	150
XLI.	Good Breeding Important in Diplomacy	154
XLII.	Great Events from Trivial Causes	161
XLIII.	"The Tongue to Persuade"	166
XLIV.	Man's Inconsistency	168
XLV.	On the *Leniores Virtutes*	174
XLVI.	The Writer's Novitiate	176
XLVII.	To acquire the Graces, etc.	180
XLVIII.	Importance of the Moral Virtues	184
XLIX.	How to Read History, etc.	187
L.	Good Manners the Source of Esteem	191
LI.	*Suaviter in Modo, Fortiter in re.*	193
LII.	*Les Bienséances*	199
LIII.	The Graces	204
LIV.	English and French Plays Compared	208
LV.	Utility of aiming at Perfection	211
LVI.	The Study of the World	215
LVII.	How History should be Written	219
LVIII.	*Avoir du Monde* Explained	221
LIX.	On Military Men. — Small Change	224
LX.	Adaptation of Manners, etc.	226
LXI.	Voltaire, Homer, Virgil, Milton, and Tasso	230
LXII.	A Worthy, Tiresome Man	234

Chesterfield's Letters to his Godson.

I.	Diversion Ordered, Study Requested, etc.	243
II.	Duty to God, and Duty to Man	244
III.	Rough Manners	246
IV.	The Well Bred Gentleman	247

CONTENTS.

LETTER		PAGE
V.	Some Rules for Behavior	248
VI.	The Art of Pleasing	250
VII.	Flat Contradiction a Proof of Ill Breeding	251
VIII.	Do unto Others as You Would they Should do unto You	253
IX.	On Self-Command	255
X.	True Wit and its Judicious Use	258
XI.	Raillery, Mimicry, Wags, and Witlings	261
XII.	The Coxcomb. — The Timid Man	263
XIII.	The Man of Spirit	266
XIV.	Vanity. — Feigned Self-Condemnation	268
XV.	Attention. — The Sense of Propriety	270
XVI.	Affections. — Polite Conversation	274
XVII.	Epitaph on a Wife	277
XVIII.	Every Man the Architect of his own Fortune	278
XIX.	Inattention. — *Hoc Age*	279
XX.	The Pride of Rank and Birth	281
XXI.	Shining Thoughts of Authors	283
XXII.	Avarice and Ambition	284
XXIII.	The Endeavor to Attain Perfection	286
XXIV.	The Treatment of Inferiors	287
XXV.	The False Pride of Rank	289
XXVI.	The Veracity of a Gentleman	291
XXVII.	On the *Je ne Sais Quoi*	293
XXVIII.	The Indecent Ostentation of Vices	295
XXIX.	The Art of Letter-Writing	296
XXX.	Treatment of Servants	298
XXXI.	Pride of Rank and Birth	299
XXXII.	The Snares of Youth	301

In applying himself to the formation of his son as a *polite man* in society, Lord Chesterfield has not given us a treatise on *duty* as Cicero has; but he has left letters which, by their mixture of justness and lightness, by certain lightsome airs which insensibly mingle with the serious graces, preserve the medium between the *Mémoires du Chevalier de Grammont* and *Télémaque*.

SAINTE-BEUVE.

Viewed as compositions, they appear almost unrivalled for a serious epistolary style.

LORD MAHON.

INTRODUCTION.

IN summarizing the character of Philip Dormer Stanhope, Earl of Chesterfield, Lecky the historian describes him as a man of "delicate but fastidious taste," "low moral principle," and "hard, keen, and worldly wisdom;" and this estimate, with an undue stress upon "low moral principle," fairly expresses the conventional idea of the brilliant eighteenth century statesman and wit. It may be said of Lord Chesterfield — and it is a rather uncommon thing to say of one of his countrymen — that his reputation has suffered more from his preaching than from his practice. Weighed fairly in the balance with his contemporaries and co-equals, he loses in great measure the invidious distinction usually bestowed upon him; and those conversant with his philosophy will readily conjecture that had he intended his preaching for the morally-sensitive ear of the British public, he would have more carefully observed his own organic maxim, — "Le Grand Art, et le plus necessaire de tous, c'est *L'Art de Plaire.*"

Lord Chesterfield's letters to his son were written in the closest confidence, with no thought to their future publication. After the death of both writer and recipient, they were published by Mrs. Eugenia Stanhope, the son's widow, as a speculative venture, — a profitable one, as it proved, the public being as ready to purchase as to condemn; and the annals of literature record few more curious turns of fortune than that which has ranked this arch-diplomat and consummate master of the art of self-repression in the category of men who have frankly confessed themselves to the world. Parental affection impelled him to discover to his son the springs of action that had governed his conduct and promoted his success in life; and the chance that led to his enduring literary fame has also installed him (with some injustice) as high priest and exemplar of fashionable vice and insincerity. To the same chance we owe our possession of a volume remarkable alike for its diction, wit, variety of argument and illustration, and keen insight into the worldly motives of worldly people. There are serious defects in Lord Chesterfield's theory of life and *savoir vivre;* but these eliminated, his system has an important advantage over many loftier ones in that it is the fruit of experience, and humanly practicable. Despite the overstrained censure of prejudice and cant, the letters have maintained their high rank in literature; and we may justly assume that their imperfections are greatly outweighed by their merits. It will be remembered that Dr. Johnson — in a lucid interval of fair-mindedness — once said of them, "Take out the immorality, and they should be put in the hands of every young gentleman;" and it is in accordance with this view of the "Great Cham of Literature" that the selections for the present volume have been made. The better to illustrate the writer's admirable epistolary style, the letters chosen are given for the most part entire; although at the risk of a leaning toward purism, we have ventured here and there to expunge expressions offensive to the delicacy of modern taste. In addition to the letters to his son, a few of the but lately published letters to his godson — written with a like purpose and from a like standpoint — are given. A hasty glance at the period in which the letters were written may serve in a measure to justify and explain their general trend and temper.

Freed from the pleasant glamor of its literary associations, English society in Lord Chesterfield's time — which we may consider as embracing the reign of Anne and those of the first two Georges — presents a repellent aspect. To the lover of the Augustan Age it is hard to realize that when Steele and Addison were chatting so charmingly in the "Tatler" and "Spectator," when Goldsmith was writing "like an angel" and the amiable Sir Joshua was behaving like one, when Pope, Swift, Fielding, Richardson, and their compeers, were on the stage, England was a sink of corruption in high places, of brutality in low. The political condition of the country for the first half-century after the revolution of 1688 was singularly provocative of venality among public men. A disputed succession, a Pretender to the throne whose title was supported by a corrupt party at home and by a profusely liberal monarch abroad, an opposing faction eager to outbid their opponents, gave rise to a complication of intrigue, a hardihood of political double and triple dealing, that caused Montesquieu to say in 1729: "Englishmen are no longer worthy of their liberty. They sell it to the King; and if the King should sell it back to them, they would sell it to him again." History has recorded, and satire and invective have rendered more odious, the faults of the leaders of the day. Marlborough, whose consummate genius broke the French prestige with an army composed of half-hearted allies and a Bardolphian home-contingent recruited largely by the parish constables, is stigmatized as "one of the basest rogues in history, supported by his mistresses, a niggard user of the pay he received from them, systematically plundering his soldiers, trafficking on political secrets, a traitor to James II., to William, to England." Vieing in baseness with the conqueror of Blenheim are Bolingbroke, the cold-blooded cynic who served and sold in turn both Queen and Pretender; the Duke of Newcastle, member of the cabinet and premier, a "living, moving, talking caricature" "whose name was perfidy;" the Earl of Mar, the Scotch Secretary of State whose exceptional rapidity of political change won for him the sobriquet of "Bobbing

John;" the profligate Wharton; Lord Hervey, the "Sporus" of Pope's malignant lines:—

> "Whether in florid impotence he speaks,
> Or as the prompter breathes the puppet squeaks;
> Or, at the ear of Eve, familiar toad,
> Half froth, half venom, spits himself abroad,
> In puns or politics, or tales or lies."

The shameful list swells at once beyond the possibility of individual mention by the addition of Walpole's packed House of Commons, where "every man had his price," and in which, Montesquieu said, "There are Scotch members who have only two hundred pounds for their vote, and who sell it for this price." England would not be England had there not been exceptions to the general rule of double-dealing and venality; and one of these exceptions it is important for us to note here. It is honorably recorded of Lord Chesterfield that he "hated a job." Of this rather untimely trait his Lordship gave signal proof during his viceroyalty in Ireland; and his biographer, Dr. Maty, relates a pleasing instance of it that occurred early in his public life. Having succeeded Lord Townshend as Captain of the Yeomen of the Guards in 1723, Lord Chesterfield was advised by his predecessor to make the post more profitable than he himself had done by disposing of the places. "I rather for this time," was the reply, "wish to follow your lordship's example than your advice."

Of the private manners of the period, the precise pencil of Hogarth and the prolific pens of a throng of satirists in prose and verse have left us the amplest memorials. If venality was the characteristic of the leaders, brutality seems to have been that of the populace; and in the turbulent and fickle mob the factious partisan found an instrument of mischief ready to his hand. When the puppet Sacheverell sounded the "drum ecclesiastic" from the pulpit of St. Paul's, the London rabble, chimney-sweepers, watermen, costermongers, thieves, flew to the rescue of the Established Church. Inflamed with gin and religious zeal, they swept through the precincts where seven years before —

"Earless on high stood unabashed Defoe,"

mobbed Defoe's fellow sectaries, and burned their meeting-houses, — at the beck of a faction who meant to enslave them. Vice wore in England so odious an aspect that one scarcely wonders when Lord Chesterfield bids his son shun the bestialities of his countrymen and adopt rather the genteel "gallantries" of the continent. Turn to Hogarth's "Gin Lane;" England's besetting sin is set forth there with all its shocking details. Gin was introduced in 1684; and half a century later, according to Lord Lonsdale's report, "England consumed seven millions of gallons." So cheap was the beverage that one could get comfortably tipsy for a penny, and dead drunk — "o'er all the ills of life victorious " — for twopence. But the ugliness, the unvarnished brutality of vice was not confined to the pleasures of the rabble. The amusements of the costermonger, so far as his money went, were the amusements of the lord. In the public resorts filth jostled finery; the blind nobleman in Hogarth's "Cockpit" bets his money freely with the ruffians about him, while the deft thief at his elbow slips a bank-note from his lordship's stake; at the bear-garden — as the "Spectator" tells us — peer and blackguard alike applauded when "Timothy Buck of Clare Market" so slashed with his broadsword his opponent "Sergeant Miller, late come from Portugal," that the latter fell disabled, and "his wound was exposed to the view of all who could delight in it, and sewed up on the stage." In the genteel revels of Hogarth's "Midnight Conversation" one sees the debauchery of "Gin Lane" minus the insignia of poverty; the company is better, the liquor is better, and the rags and tatters are replaced by bands and cassocks, lace and ruffles, cocked hats and full-bottomed wigs; but the essentials are the same, and the gentlemen — from the divine who presides at the punch-bowl to the officer who sprawls on the floor — exhibit every stage of the national vice. England in the eighteenth century was not, as Lord Chesterfield said, "the home of The Graces."

That polite society at this period was lax in its morals, that "a mistress was as well recognized as a concubine in the days of King David," is scarcely to be wondered at when we consider the precedent of royalty. The domestic annals of the royal contemners of "boetry and bainting," George I. and George II., read very much like those of Macheath and his gang. There was no concealment in these delicate matters at that time; the facts were as plain as noonday, and it was thought no scandal that an officer should owe his rank, or a prelate his lawn, to the good offices of the Duchess of Kendal or of Madam Walmoden. Certainly there is little to be said in extenuation of the immorality of a class that can enjoy, laugh at, and applaud a bitterly truthful satire on its own vices. In his "Beggar's Opera" Gay exhibited to polite society the reflection of its own detestable manners mirrored in the annals of a band of thieves and prostitutes; and polite society, instead of slitting the ears of the author, made much of him, and rapturously admitted the fidelity of the portrait.

Such, broadly speaking, were the social externals in England when Lord Chesterfield lived; and it is by the temper of his time and country that he is to be judged. Few men will bear comparison with the standards of an age more advanced than their own. The defects of Chesterfield — as Lord Mahon says — were "neither slight nor few." He was addicted to gaming; he carried flattery and dissimulation beyond justifiable bounds; and neither his life nor his precept was free from the taint of the prevailing immorality. Much of the common estimate of

Lord Chesterfield has been founded on Dr. Johnson's opinion, — and Dr. Johnson's opinion where his prejudices were engaged was usually worthless. The story of his quarrel with the Earl is well known, and the facts lie in a nutshell. On the one hand was Lord Chesterfield, a leader in society, literature, and politics, a man whose name was a synonym for good breeding, and in whose eyes the graces and amenities of life were of paramount importance; on the other was Dr. Johnson, a phenomenon of learning and intellectual force, but also, unhappily, a phenomenon of slovenliness, ill breeding, and personal repulsiveness. Assuming human nature to have been, in the main, what it is to-day, we can scarcely blame Lord Chesterfield for declining the intimacy of one who must have been peculiarly repugnant to him. Much solemn nonsense in the way of moral dissertation has grown out of the story that he once kept Johnson waiting in an antechamber — Lord Lyttleton places the time at ten minutes — while he chatted with so frivolous a person as Colley Cibber. There is little doubt that the Earl found Cibber's lively prattle more entertaining than the ponderous "Sirs!" of the Doctor; and we may believe that so fastidious a nobleman objected to being knocked down with the butt of Johnson's conversational pistol, — which was Goldsmith's figurative way of saying that when the Doctor was fairly worsted in an argument he silenced his opponent with a roar of abuse or a staggering sophistry. Is it not curious that posterity has been so unwilling to condone Lord Chesterfield's shadowy discourtesy toward one whose habitual bearishness toward all was proverbial?

It is not my intention here to go into the details of Lord Chesterfield's career. It may be well, however, to recapitulate the leading facts before turning to a brief consideration of his letters. He was born in London on Sept. 22, 1694, and in 1712 he entered Trinity Hall, Cambridge. After two years of close application at Cambridge, he visited the Hague, where he served his novitiate in polite society, frequenting the best companies and adding to his solid attainments those lighter arts in which he afterwards excelled, and by means of which he declared that he sought to make "every woman love and every man admire" him. In 1715, upon the accession of George I., he became Gentleman of the Bed Chamber to the Prince of Wales, and shortly after entered the House of Commons. In 1726 he was called to the House of Peers by the death of his father. Oratory had been his chief study, and here he found himself in a theatre suited to the refined and studied eloquence in which he easily surpassed his compeers. The grace of manner, refined wit, and facility in classical allusion, which failed to touch the more popular assembly, were here relished and applauded. Horace Walpole, who had heard the first orators of his day, declared that the finest speech he had ever listened to was one from Chesterfield. In 1727 he was sent as ambassador to Holland; and it was during his stay at the Hague that he met the lady, Madam de Bouchet, who became, in 1732, the mother of his son, to whom the most of the letters in this volume are addressed. In 1733 he married Melusina de Schulemberg, niece of the Duchess of Kendal, — or as some said, her daughter by George I. In 1744 he was again sent as envoy to the Hague, and in the following year he entered on his memorable Lord Lieutenancy in Ireland. Although Lord Chesterfield's public engagements were uniformly fulfilled with credit to himself and with satisfaction to his countrymen, his term in Ireland was undoubtedly the most brilliant and useful part of his career. It is not too much to say that at no time in the history of that hapless country has English rule been so well administered. To please or even to content the Irish people is for the English representative a task that dwarfs the labors of Hercules; yet we learn that at the close of Lord Chesterfield's administration "persons of all ranks and religions followed him to the water's edge, praising and blessing him, and entreating him to return." It will be remembered that when Lord Chesterfield went to Dublin in 1745 he was confronted with unusual difficulties. Politically, the period was one of transition; time had not yet ratified the title of a dynasty toward which the Irish were generally disaffected, and the adherents of a claimant whom they generally favored were up in arms in the neighboring island. Though eminently satisfactory to both factions, Lord Chesterfield's policy in Ireland was one of most unwavering firmness, and was not without severity when called for. It is related that he said to a supposed agent of the Pretender: "Sir, I do not wish to inquire whether you have any particular employment in this kingdom, but I know you have great influence among those of your persuasion. I have sent for you to exhort them to be peaceable and quiet. If they behave like faithful subjects they shall be treated as such, but if they act in a different manner, I will be worse to them than Cromwell." In 1746 Lord Chesterfield became Secretary of State, resigning in 1748. He had long been troubled with deafness, and in 1755, his infirmity becoming so serious as to incapacitate him from taking part in public affairs, he determined to go into retirement. His death occurred on March 24, 1773, five years after that of the son upon whom he had bestowed such a wealth of care and affection.

Lord Chesterfield's letters to his son have been strongly reprehended on three distinct grounds: first, because their teachings are sometimes immoral; secondly, because of the seemingly undue stress placed upon good breeding and the graces; and thirdly, because the maxims, even when good in themselves, seldom rest on higher grounds than expediency or personal advantage.

Lord Chesterfield's most determined panegyrist

will scarcely deny that some of his precepts are, in themselves, inexcusably bad. But where is the source, the well-spring, of these precepts? Not, I think, in the heart of the writer. "Let us first" — as Johnson once said to Boswell — "clear our minds of cant," and then consider that it was not his son's prospects in the next world but his welfare in this that the anxious father deemed himself qualified to advance; and of his intimate and curious knowledge of the ways of this world there is no doubt. Lord Chesterfield would scarcely have presented the "Letters" to the world as embodying a system of absolute ethics. Long years of acute watching and deliberate weighing of the preferences and foibles of his fellows convinced him that to appear well in their eyes, — or, as he expressed it, "to make people in general wish him well, and inclined to serve him in anything not inconsistent with their own interests," — he must act in such and such a way; and in that he unshrinkingly put certain pitiful results of his experience of men and women into the form of advice to his son, lies the essence of his fault. We are not, however, to hold the observer responsible for the phenomena from which he drew his conclusions.

As to the second objection to the letters, the answer must be obvious to all who consider for a moment their nature and the purpose with which they were composed. They were written, not for the public, but for the instruction of an individual;

and naturally stress is laid upon those qualities and acquirements in which that individual was deficient. Mr. Stanhope was naturally studious, hence we find comparatively little insistence upon the more solid attainments; Mr. Stanhope was inclined to be moral, hence his father did not insult him by constantly referring to the Decalogue; but Mr. Stanhope was naturally somewhat *distrait* and awkward, hence Lord Chesterfield wrote, "For God's sake, therefore, think of nothing but shining and even distinguishing yourself in the most polite courts by your air, your address, your manners, your politeness, your *douceur*, your graces."

There are very few of us, I think, who will venture to quarrel with Lord Chesterfield on the grounds stated in the third objection, if we steadily bear in mind Dr. Johnson's excellent advice on the subject of cant.

Before closing this hasty sketch a word should be added regarding the series of letters which form the concluding portion of the present volume, and of the person to whom they were addressed. With a few exceptions, it is only within the current year that Lord Chesterfield's letters to his godson have been given to the public; and we have gladly availed ourselves of the opportunity of adding to our collection an element of such freshness and interest. The literary value of these later letters will be taken for granted. The qualities that secured for Lord Chesterfield's letters to his son their high rank in epistolary literature are not of course wanting in those to his godson, written with a like general purpose. There is however a perceptible difference between the two sets, owing in part to the advanced years of the writer, in part to the extreme youth of the recipient. To many readers the flagging of the old intellectual fire and acuteness noticeable in the letters to the godson will be compensated by their kindlier, more liberal, and less worldly tone. In both series will be found the same frequent insistence upon the importance of manners and the graces, and this is largely due to the fact that son and godson were strikingly alike in general character and disposition; both were studiously inclined and of good habits, and both were shy of those divinities to whose altar their Mentor so constantly urged them. Philip Stanhope, the godson, was the son of Arthur Charles Stanhope of Mansfield, a somewhat distant relative of Lord Chesterfield, and was adopted by him, upon his son's death, as heir to his rank, fortune, and affections. Like the son, the godson failed to fulfil the brilliant hopes formed of him; and instead of the shining diplomat, statesman, and courtier, he seems to have turned out the humdrum, quite commonplace country gentleman, — a respectable man but by no means a votary of the Graces. Madame d'Arblay wrote of him: "How would that quintessence of high ton, the late Lord Chesterfield, blush to behold his successor, who with much share of humor and of good humor also, has as little good breeding as any man I ever met with."

As before intimated, it is the aim of the projectors of this volume to show Lord Chesterfield at his best; to select from the mass of his letters those that are in themselves the most valuable, — a process which has obliged us occasionally to reject letters and expunge passages which the writer's detractors would perhaps deem specially characteristic of him. We have, however, we believe, prepared a volume that will prove not only useful and readable, but morally unobjectionable; and if our general aim has been attained, there are few readers who will not feel repaid for the perusal of the following pages.

E. G. J.

LETTERS OF LORD CHESTERFIELD TO HIS SON.

LETTERS OF LORD CHESTERFIELD TO HIS SON.

I.

GOOD BREEDING RELATIVE AND GENERAL. — *MAUVAISE HONTE.*

Wednesday.[1]

DEAR BOY, — You behaved yourself so well at Mr. Boden's last Sunday that you justly deserve commendation; besides, you encourage me to give you some rules of politeness and good breeding, being persuaded that you will observe them. Know then that as learning, honor, and virtue are absolutely necessary to gain you the esteem and admiration of mankind, politeness and good breeding are equally necessary to make you welcome and agreeable in conversation and common life. Great talents, such as honor, virtue, learning, and parts, are above the generality of the world, who neither possess them themselves nor judge of them rightly in others; but

---

[1] At the time this was written, Master Stanhope was in his ninth year. The letter following was written a few months later.

all people are judges of the lesser talents, such as civility, affability, and an obliging, agreeable address and manner, because they feel the good effects of them as making society easy and pleasing. Good sense must in many cases determine good breeding; because the same thing that would be civil at one time, and to one person, may be quite otherwise at another time, and to another person; but there are some general rules of good breeding that hold always true, and in all cases. As, for example, it is always extremely rude to answer only Yes, or No, to anybody, without adding Sir, My Lord, or Madam, according to the quality of the person you speak to, — as in French you must always say, Monsieur, Milord, Madame, and Mademoiselle. I suppose you know that every married woman is in French Madame, and every unmarried one is Mademoiselle. It is likewise extremely rude not to give the proper attention and a civil answer when people speak to you, or to go away, or be doing something else, when they are speaking to you; for that convinces them that you despise them, and do not think it worth your while to hear or answer what they say. I dare say I need not tell you how rude it is to take the best place in a room, or to seize immediately upon what you like at table, without offering first to help others, — as if you considered nobody but yourself. On the contrary, you should always endeavor to procure all the conveniences you can to the people you are with. Besides being civil, which is absolutely necessary, the perfection of good breeding is to be civil with ease, and in a gentleman-like manner.

For this, you should observe the French people, who excel in it, and whose politeness seems as easy and natural as any other part of their conversation; whereas the English are often awkward in their civilities, and when they mean to be civil, are too much ashamed to get it out. But, pray, do you remember never to be ashamed of doing what is right; you would have a great deal of reason to be ashamed if you were not civil, but what reason can you have to be ashamed of being civil? And why not say a civil and obliging thing as easily and as naturally as you would ask what o'clock it is? This kind of bashfulness, which is justly called by the French *mauvaise honte*, is the distinguishing character of an English booby, who is frightened out of his wits when people of fashion speak to him; and when he is to answer them, blushes, stammers, and can hardly get out what he would say, and becomes really ridiculous from a groundless fear of being laughed at; whereas a real well-bred man would speak to all the kings in the world with as little concern and as much ease as he would speak to you.

Remember, then, that to be civil, and to be civil with ease (which is properly called good breeding), is the only way to be beloved and well received in company; that to be ill bred and rude is intolerable, and the way to be kicked out of company; and that to be bashful is to be ridiculous. As I am sure you will mind and practise all this, I expect that when you are *novennis*, you will not only be the best scholar but the best-bred boy in England of your age. Adieu.

II.

A GENTEEL MANNER IMPORTANT. — AN AWKWARD FELLOW. — ATTENTION.

SPA, *July* 25, N. S. 1741.

DEAR BOY, — I have often told you in my former letters — and it is most certainly true — that the strictest and most scrupulous honor and virtue can alone make you esteemed and valued by mankind; that parts and learning can alone make you admired and celebrated by them; but that the possession of lesser talents was most absolutely necessary towards making you liked, beloved, and sought after in private life. Of these lesser talents, good breeding is the principal and most necessary one, not only as it is very important in itself, but as it adds great lustre to the more solid advantages both of the heart and the mind. I have often touched upon good breeding to you before, so that this letter shall be upon the next necessary qualification to it, which is a genteel and easy manner and carriage, wholly free from those odd tricks, ill habits, and awkwardnesses, which even many very worthy and sensible people have in their behavior. However trifling a genteel manner may sound, it is of very great consequence towards pleasing in private life, especially the women, which one time or other you will think worth pleasing; and I have known many a man from his awkwardness give people such a dislike of him at first that all his merit could not get the better of it afterwards. Whereas a genteel manner prepossesses people in your favor, bends them towards you, and makes them wish to be like you. Awkwardness can proceed but from two causes, — either from not having kept good company, or from not having attended to it. As for your keeping good company, I will take care of that ; do you take care to observe their ways and manners, and to form your own upon them. Attention is absolutely necessary for this, as indeed it is for everything else ; and a man without attention is not fit to live in the world. When an awkward fellow first comes into a room, it is highly probable that his sword gets between his legs and throws him down, or makes him stumble at least ; when he has recovered this accident, he goes and places himself in the very place of the whole room where he should not ; there he soon lets his hat fall down, and in taking it up again throws down his cane ; in recovering his cane, his hat falls a second time, so that he is a quarter of an hour before he is in order again. If he drinks tea or coffee, he certainly scalds his mouth, and lets either the cup or the saucer fall, and spills either the tea or coffee in his breeches. At dinner, his awkwardness distinguishes itself particularly, as he has more to do ; there he holds his knife, fork, and spoon differently from other people, eats with his knife, to the great danger of his mouth, picks his teeth with his fork, and puts his spoon into the dishes again. If he is to carve he can never hit the joint, but in his vain efforts to cut through the bone scatters the sauce in everybody's face. He generally daubs himself with soup and grease, though his napkin is commonly stuck through a button-hole and tickles his chin. When he drinks, he infallibly coughs in his glass and besprinkles the company. . . . His hands are troublesome to him when he has not something in them, and he does not know where to put them; but they are in perpetual motion between his bosom and his breeches; he does not wear his clothes, and in short does nothing, like other people. All this, I own, is not in any degree criminal; but it is highly disagreeable and ridiculous in company, and ought most carefully to be avoided by whoever desires to please.

From this account of what you should not do, you may easily judge what you should do; and a due attention to the manners of people of fashion, and who have seen the world, will make it habitual and familiar to you.

There is, likewise, an awkwardness of expression and words most carefully to be avoided, — such as false English, bad pronunciation, old sayings, and common proverbs, which are so many proofs of having kept bad and low company. For example : if, instead of saying that tastes are different and that every man has his own peculiar one, you should let off a proverb, and say, That what is one man's meat is another man's poison; or else, Every one as they like, as the good man said when he kissed his cow, — everybody would be persuaded that you had never kept company with anybody above footmen and housemaids.

Attention will do all this; and without attention nothing is to be done : want of attention, which is really want of thought, is either folly or madness. You should not only have attention to everything but a quickness of attention, so as to observe at once all the people in the room, their motions, their looks, and their words, and yet without staring at them and seeming to be an observer. This quick and unobserved observation is of infinite advantage in life, and is to be acquired with care; and on the contrary what is called absence, which is thoughtlessness and want of attention about what is doing, makes a man so like either a fool or a madman, that for my part I see no real difference. A fool never has thought; a madman has lost it; and an absent man is, for the time, without it.

. . . .

III.

TRUE PRAISE.—ELEMENTARY POLITENESS.

SPA, *Aug.* 6, 1741.

DEAR BOY,—I am very well pleased with the several performances you sent me, and still more so with Mr. Maittaire's letter that accompanied them, in which he gives me a much better account of you than he did in his former. *Laudari a laudato viro* was always a commendable ambition; encourage that ambition, and continue to deserve the praises of the praiseworthy. While you do so, you shall have whatever you will from me; and when you cease to do so, you shall have nothing.

I am glad you have begun to compose a little; it will give you a habit of thinking upon subjects, which is at least as necessary as reading them; therefore pray send me your thoughts upon this subject, —

"Non sibi, sed toti genitum se credere mundo."

It is a part of Cato's character in Lucan, who says that Cato did not think himself born for himself only, but for all mankind. Let me know, then, whether you think that a man is born only for his own pleasure and advantage, or whether he is not obliged to contribute to the good of the society in which he lives and of all mankind in general. This is certain, — that every man receives advantages from society which he could not have if he were the only man in the world: therefore is he not in some measure in debt to society; and is he not obliged to do for others what they do for him? You may do this in English or Latin, which you please; for it is the thinking part, and not the language, that I mind in this case.

I warned you in my last against those disagreeable tricks and awkwardnesses which many people contract when they are young by the negligence of their parents, and cannot get quit of them when they are old, — such as odd motions, strange postures, and ungenteel carriage. But there is likewise an awkwardness of the mind that ought to be and with care may be avoided; as, for instance, to mistake names. To speak of Mr. What-d'ye-call-him or Mrs. Thingum or How-d'ye-call-her is excessively awkward and ordinary. To call people by improper titles and appellations is so too; as my Lord for Sir, and Sir for my Lord. To begin a story or narration when you are not perfect in it and cannot go through with it, but are forced possibly to say in the middle of it, "I have forgot the rest," is very unpleasant and bungling. One must be extremely exact, clear, and perspicuous in everything one says; otherwise instead of entertaining or informing others, one only tires and puzzles them. The voice and manner of speaking, too, are not to be neglected. Some people almost shut their mouths when they speak and mutter so that they are not to be understood; others speak so fast and sputter that they are not to be understood neither; some always speak as loud as if they were talking to deaf people; and others so low that one cannot hear them. All these habits are awkward and disagreeable, and are to be avoided by attention; they are the distinguishing marks of the ordinary people who have had no care taken of their education. You cannot imagine how necessary it is to mind all these little things; for I have seen many people with great talents ill received for want of having these talents too, and others well received only from their little talents, and who had no great ones. Adieu.

IV.

DANCING.—ALL THINGS, EVEN TRIFLES, SHOULD BE DONE WELL.

DUBLIN CASTLE, *Nov.* 19, 1745.[1]

DEAR BOY,— . . . Now that the Christmas breaking-up draws near, I have ordered Mr. Desnoyers to go to you during that time, to teach you to dance. I desire you will particularly attend to the graceful motion of your arms, which with the manner of putting on your hat and giving your hand is all that a gentleman need attend to. Dancing is in itself a very trifling, silly thing; but it is one of those established follies to which people of sense are sometimes obliged to conform, and then they should be able to do it well. And though I would not have you a dancer, yet when you do dance I would have you dance well, as I would have you do everything you do well. There is no one thing so trifling but which, if it is to be done at all, ought to be done well; and I have often told you that I wished you even played at pitch and cricket better than any boy at Westminster. For instance, dress is a very foolish thing, and yet it is a very foolish thing for a man not to be well dressed, according to his rank and way of life; and it is so far from being a disparagement to any man's understanding that it is rather a proof of it to be as well dressed as those whom he lives with: the difference in this case between a man of sense and a fop is that the fop

[1] Written during Lord Chesterfield's viceroyalty in Ireland.

values himself upon his dress, and the man of sense laughs at it, at the same time that he knows he must not neglect it. There are a thousand foolish customs of this kind, which, not being criminal, must be complied with, and even cheerfully, by men of sense. Diogenes the cynic was a wise man for despising them, but a fool for showing it. Be wiser than other people, if you can; but do not tell them so.

. . . .

V.

ELOCUTION: METHOD OF DEMOSTHENES.

DUBLIN CASTLE, *Feb.* 8, 1746.

. . . .

YOU propose, I find, Demosthenes for your model, and you have chosen very well; but remember the pains he took to be what he was. He spoke near the sea in storms, both to use himself to speak aloud, and not to be disturbed by the noise and tumult of public assemblies; he put stones in his mouth to help his elocution, which naturally was not advantageous; from which facts I conclude, that whenever he spoke he opened both his lips and his teeth, and that he articulated every word and every syllable distinctly, and full loud enough to be heard the whole length of my library.

As he took so much pains for the graces of oratory only, I conclude he took still more for the more solid parts of it. I am apt to think he applied himself extremely to the propriety, the purity, and the elegance of his language; to the distribution of the parts of his oration; to the force of his arguments; to the strength of his proofs; and to the passions as well as the judgments of his audience. I fancy he began with an *exordium*, to gain the good opinion and the affections of his audience; that afterwards he stated the point in question briefly but clearly; that he then brought his proofs, afterwards his arguments; and that he concluded with a *peroratio*, in which he recapitulated the whole succinctly, enforced the strong parts, and artfully slipped over the weak ones; and at last made his strong push at the passions of his hearers. Wherever you would persuade or prevail, address yourself to the passions; it is by them that mankind is to be taken. Caesar bade his soldiers at the battle of Pharsalia aim at the faces of Pompey's men; they did so, and prevailed. I bid you strike at the passions; and if you do, you too will prevail. If you can once engage people's pride, love, pity, ambition, — or whichever is their prevailing passion, — on your side, you need not fear what their reason can do against you.

. . . .

VI.

INATTENTION. — KNOWLEDGE OF MANKIND.

DUBLIN CASTLE, *March* 10, 1746.

SIR, — I most thankfully acknowledge the honor of two or three letters from you, since 1 troubled you with my last; and am very proud of the repeated instances you give me of your favor and protection, which I shall endeavor to deserve.[1]

I am very glad that you went to hear a trial in the Court of King's Bench; and still more so, that you made the proper animadversions upon the inattention of many of the people in the Court. As you observed very well the indecency of that inattention, I am sure you will never be guilty of anything like it yourself. There is no surer sign in the world of a little, weak mind than inattention. Whatever is worth doing at all is worth doing well; and nothing can be well done without attention. It is the sure answer of a fool, when you ask him about anything that was said or done where he was present, that "truly he did not mind it." And why did not the fool mind it? What had he else to do there but to mind what was doing? A man of sense sees, hears, and retains everything that passes where he is. I desire I may never hear you talk of not minding, nor complain, as most fools do, of a treacherous memory. Mind not only what people say but how they say it; and if you have any sagacity, you may discover more truth by your eyes than by your ears. People can say what they will, but they cannot look just as they will; and their looks frequently discover what their words are calculated to conceal. Observe, therefore, people's looks carefully when they speak, not only to you, but to each other. I have often guessed by people's

[1] A little badinage at the expense of the boy, who at that date was about fourteen.

faces what they were saying, though I could not hear one word they said. The most material knowledge of all — I mean the knowledge of the world — is never to be acquired without great attention; and I know many old people, who though they have lived long in the world, are but children still as to the knowledge of it, from their levity and inattention. Certain forms which all people comply with, and certain arts which all people aim at, hide in some degree the truth and give a general exterior resemblance to almost everybody. Attention and sagacity must see through that veil and discover the natural character. You are of an age now to reflect, to observe and compare characters, and to arm yourself against the common arts, — at least of the world. If a man with whom you are but barely acquainted, and to whom you have made no offers nor given any marks of friendship, makes you on a sudden strong professions of his, receive them with civility, but do not repay them with confidence; he certainly means to deceive you, for one man does not fall in love with another at sight. If a man uses strong protestations or oaths to make you believe a thing which is of itself so likely and probable that the bare saying of it would be sufficient, depend upon it he lies, and is highly interested in making you believe it; or else he would not take so much pains.

In about five weeks I propose having the honor of laying myself at your feet, — which I hope to find grown longer than they were when I left them. Adieu.

VII.

NEVER ATTACK A CORPS COLLECTIVELY.

April 5, 1746.

DEAR BOY, — Before it is very long, I am of opinion that you will both think and speak more favorably of women than you do now. You seem to think that from Eve downwards they have done a great deal of mischief. As for that lady, I give her up to you; but since her time, history will inform you that men have done much more mischief in the world than women; and to say the truth, I would not advise you to trust either more than is absolutely necessary. But this I will advise you to, which is, never to attack whole bodies of any kind; for besides that all general rules have their exceptions, you unnecessarily make yourself a great number of enemies by attacking a *corps* collectively. Among women, as among men, there are good as well as bad; and it may be full as many or more good than among men. This rule holds as to lawyers, soldiers, parsons, courtiers, citizens, etc. They are all men, subject to the same passions and sentiments, differing only in the manner, according to their several educations; and it would be as imprudent as unjust to attack any of them by the lump. Individuals forgive sometimes; but bodies and societies never do. Many young people think it very genteel and witty to abuse the clergy; in which they are extremely mistaken, since in my opinion parsons are very like men, and neither the better nor the worse for wearing a black gown. All general reflections upon nations and societies are the trite, threadbare jokes of those who set up for wit without having any, and so have recourse to commonplace. Judge of individuals from your own knowledge of them, and not from their sex, profession, or denomination.

. . . .

VIII.

ON TRAVELLING INTELLIGENTLY. — THE WELL-BRED TRAVELLER.

BATH, *Sept.* 29, O. S. 1746.[1]

DEAR BOY, — I received by the last mail your letter of the 23d N. S. from Heidelberg, and am very well pleased to find that you inform yourself of the particulars of the several places you go through. You do mighty right to see the curiosities in those several places, such as the Golden Bull at Frankfort, the Tun at Heidelberg, etc. Other travellers see and talk of them; it is very proper to see them, too, but remember that seeing is the least material object of travelling, — hearing and knowing are the essential points. Therefore pray let your inquiries be chiefly directed to the knowledge of the constitution and

---

[1] At this date Mr. Stanhope was making his continental tour in quest of " The Graces."

particular customs of the places where you either reside at or pass through, whom they belong to, by what right and tenure, and since when; in whom the supreme authority is lodged; and by what magistrates, and in what manner, the civil and criminal justice is administered. It is likewise necessary to get as much acquaintance as you can, in order to observe the characters and manners of the people; for though human nature is in truth the same through the whole human species, yet it is so differently modified and varied by education, habit, and different customs, that one should, upon a slight and superficial observation, almost think it different.

As I have never been in Switzerland myself, I must desire you to inform me, now and then, of the constitution of that country. As, for instance, do the Thirteen Cantons jointly and collectively form one government where the supreme authority is lodged, or is each canton sovereign in itself, and under no tie or constitutional obligation of acting in common concert with the other cantons? Can any one canton make war or form an alliance with a foreign power without the consent of the other twelve or at least a majority of them? Can one canton declare war against another? If every canton is sovereign and independent in itself, in whom is the supreme power of that canton lodged? Is it in one man, or in a certain number of men? If in one man, what is he called? If in a number, what are they called,— Senate, Council, or what? I do not suppose that you can yet know these things yourself; but a very little inquiry of those who do will enable you to answer me these few questions in your next. You see, I am sure, the necessity of knowing these things thoroughly, and consequently the necessity of conversing much with the people of the country, who alone can inform you rightly; whereas, most of the English who travel converse only with each other, and consequently know no more when they return to England than they did when they left it. This proceeds from a *mauvaise honte* which makes them ashamed of going into company; and frequently, too, from the want of the necessary language (French) to enable them to bear their part in it. As for the *mauvaise honte*, I hope you are above it. Your figure is like other people's; I suppose you will care that your dress shall be so, too, and to avoid any singularity. What, then, should you be ashamed of, and why not go into a mixed company with as much ease and as little concern as you would go into your own room? Vice and ignorance are the only things I know which one ought to be ashamed of; keep but clear of them and you may go anywhere without fear or concern. I have known some people who, from feeling the pain and inconveniences of this *mauvaise honte*, have rushed into the other extreme and turned impudent, as cowards sometimes grow desperate from the excess of danger; but this, too, is carefully to be avoided, there being nothing more generally shocking than impudence. The medium between these two extremes marks out the well-bred man; he feels himself firm and easy in all companies; is modest without being bashful, and steady without being impudent; if he is a stranger, he observes with care the manners and ways of the people most esteemed at that place, and conforms to them with complaisance. Instead of finding fault with the customs of that place and telling the people that the English ones are a thousand times better, — as my countrymen are very apt to do, — he commends their table, their dress, their houses, and their manners a little more, it may be, than he really thinks they deserve. But this degree of complaisance is neither criminal nor abject, and is but a small price to pay for the good-will and affection of the people you converse with. As the generality of people are weak enough to be pleased with these little things, those who refuse to please them so cheaply are, in my mind, weaker than they.

. . . .

IX.

THE "ABSENT MAN."—THOUGHTFULNESS.

BATH, *Oct.* 9, O. S. 1746.

DEAR BOY, —

. . . .

What is commonly called an absent man is commonly either a very weak or a very affected man; but be he which he will, he is, I am sure, a very disagreeable man in company. He fails in all the common offices of civility; he seems not to know those people to-day whom yesterday he appeared to live in intimacy with; he takes no part in the general conversation, but on the contrary breaks into it from time to time with some start of his own, as if he waked from a dream. This (as I said before) is a sure indication either of a mind so weak that it is not able to bear above one object at a time, or so affected that it would be supposed to be wholly engrossed by and directed to some very great and important objects. Sir Isaac Newton, Mr. Locke, and (it may be) five or six more, since the creation of the world, may have had a right to absence, from that intense thought which the things they were investigating required. But if a young man, and a man of the world, who has no such avocations to plead, will claim and exercise that right of absence in company, his pretended right should in my mind be turned into an involuntary absence by his perpetual exclusion out of company. However frivolous a company may be, still while you are among them, do not show them by your inattention that you think them so; but rather take their tone, and conform in some degree to their weakness, instead of manifesting your contempt for them. There is nothing that people bear more impatiently or forgive less than contempt; and an injury is much sooner forgotten than an insult. If therefore you would rather please than offend, rather be well than ill spoken of, rather be loved than hated, remember to have that constant attention about you which flatters every man's little vanity, and the want of which, by mortifying his pride, never fails to excite his resentment or at least his ill will. For instance, most people (I might say all people) have their weaknesses; they have their aversions and their likings to such or such things; so that if you were to laugh at a man for his aversion to a cat or cheese (which are common antipathies), or by inattention and negligence to let them come in his way where you could prevent it, he would in the first case think himself insulted and in the second slighted, and would remember both. Whereas your care to procure for him what he likes and to remove from him what he hates, shows him that he is at least an object of your attention; flatters his vanity, and makes him possibly more your friend than a more important service would have done. With regard to women, attentions still below these are necessary, and by the custom of the world, in some measure due, according to the laws of good breeding.

My long and frequent letters, which I send you in great doubt of their success, put me in mind of certain papers, which you have very lately, and I formerly, sent up to kites along the string, which we called messengers; some of them the wind used to blow away, others were torn by the string, and but few of them got up and stuck to the kite. But I will content myself now, as I did then, if some of my present messengers do but stick to you. Adieu!

X.

TRUE PLEASURE INCONSISTENT WITH VICE.

LONDON, *March* 27, O. S. 1747.

DEAR BOY, — Pleasure is the rock which most young people split upon. They launch out with crowded sails in quest of it, but without a compass to direct their course, or reason sufficient to steer the vessel; for want of which, pain and shame, instead of pleasure, are the returns of their voyage. Do not think that I mean to snarl at pleasure like a Stoic, or to preach against it like a parson; no, I mean to point it out, and recommend it to you, like an Epicurean. I wish you a great deal, and my only view is to hinder you from mistaking it.

The character which most young men first aim at is that of a man of pleasure; but they generally take it upon trust, and instead of consulting their own taste and inclinations, they blindly adopt whatever those with whom they chiefly converse are pleased to call by the name of pleasure; and a *man of pleasure*, in the vulgar acceptation of that phrase, means only a beastly drunkard, an abandoned rake, and a profligate swearer and curser. As it may be of use to you, I am not unwilling, though at the same time ashamed, to own that the vices of my youth proceeded much more from my silly resolution of being what I heard called a Man of Pleasure than from my own inclinations. I always naturally hated drinking; and yet I have often drunk, with disgust at the time, attended by great sickness the next day, only because I then considered drinking as a necessary qualification for a fine gentleman and a Man of Pleasure.

The same as to gaming. I did not want money, and consequently had no occasion to play for it; but I thought play another necessary ingredient in the composition of a Man of Pleasure, and accordingly I plunged into it without desire at first, sacrificed a thousand real pleasures to it, and made myself solidly uneasy by it for thirty the best years of my life.

I was even absurd enough for a little while to swear, by way of adorning and completing the shining character which I affected; but this folly I soon laid aside upon finding both the guilt and the indecency of it.

Thus seduced by fashion, and blindly adopting nominal pleasures, I lost real ones; and my fortune impaired and my constitution shattered are, I must confess, the just punishment of my errors.

Take warning then by them; choose your pleasures for yourself, and do not let them be imposed upon you. Follow Nature, and not fashion; weigh the present enjoyment of your pleasures against the necessary consequences of them, and then let your own common-sense determine your choice.

Were I to begin the world again with the experience which I now have of it, I would lead a life of real not of imaginary pleasure. I would enjoy the pleasures of the table and of wine, but stop short of the pains inseparably annexed to an excess in either. I would not, at twenty years, be a preaching missionary of abstemiousness and sobriety, and I should let other people do as they would without formally and sententiously rebuking them for it; but I would be most firmly resolved not to destroy my own faculties and constitution in compliance to those who have no regard to their own. I would play to give me pleasure, but not to give me pain; that is, I would play for trifles, in mixed companies, to amuse myself and conform to custom; but I would take care not to venture for sums which, if I won, I should not be the better for, but if I lost, should be under a difficulty to pay, and when paid would oblige me to retrench in several other articles, — not to mention the quarrels which deep play commonly occasions.

I would pass some of my time in reading and the rest in the company of people of sense and learning, and chiefly those above me; and I would frequent the mixed companies of men and women of fashion, which, though often frivolous, yet they unbend and refresh the mind, not uselessly because they certainly polish and soften the manners.

• • • • • • • • •

XI.

A SHOWY BINDING. — TRUE ATTIC SALT.

LONDON, *April* 3, O. S. 1747.

DEAR BOY, — If I am rightly informed, I am now writing to a fine gentleman in a scarlet coat laced with gold, a brocade waistcoat, and all other suitable ornaments. The natural partiality of every author for his own works makes me very glad to hear that Mr. Harte has thought this last edition of mine worth so fine a binding; and as he has bound it in red and gilt it upon the back, I hope he will take care that it shall be *lettered* too. A showish binding attracts the eyes, and engages the attention of everybody, — but with this difference, that women, and men who are like women, mind the binding more than the book; whereas men of sense and learning immediately examine the inside, and if they find that it does not answer the finery on the outside, they throw it by with the greater indignation and contempt. I hope that when this edition of my works shall be opened and read, the best judges will find connection, consistency, solidity, and spirit in it. Mr. Harte may *recensere* and *emendare* as much as he pleases; but it will be to little purpose, if you do not co-operate with him. The work will be imperfect. . . .

I like your account of the salt-works, which shows that you gave some attention while you were seeing them. But notwithstanding that by your account the Swiss salt is (I dare say) very good, yet I am apt to suspect that it falls a little short of the true Attic salt, in which there was a peculiar quickness and delicacy. That same Attic salt seasoned almost all Greece except Bœotia; and a great deal of it was exported afterwards to Rome, where it was counterfeited by a composition called Urbanity, which in some time was brought to very near the perfection of the original Attic salt. The more you are powdered with these two kinds of salt, the better you will keep and the more you will be relished.

XII.

EPISTOLARY MODELS.

LONDON, *July* 20, O. S. 1747

. . . *Apropos* of letter-writing, the best models that you can form yourself upon are Cicero, Cardinal d'Ossat, Madame Sevigné, and Comte Bussy Rabutin. Cicero's Epistles to Atticus, and to his familiar friends, are the best examples that you can imitate in the friendly and the familiar style. The simplicity and the clearness of Cardinal d'Ossat's letters show how letters of business ought to be written; no affected turns, no attempts at wit obscure or perplex his matter, which is always plainly and clearly stated, as business always should be. For gay and amusing letters, for *enjouement* and *badinage*, there are none that equal Comte Bussy's and Madame Sevigné's. They are so natural that they seem to be the extempore conversations of two people of wit, rather than letters, — which are commonly studied, though they ought not to be so. I would advise you to let that book be one in your itinerant library; it will both amuse and inform you.

· · · · · · · · · ·

XIII.

TOLERANCE AND TRUTH RECOMMENDED.

LONDON, *Sept.* 21, O. S. 1747.

DEAR BOY, — I received by the last post your letter of the 8th, N. S., and I do not wonder that you are surprised at the credulity and superstition of the Papists at Einsiedlen, and at their absurd stories of their chapel. But remember at the same time that errors and mistakes, however gross, in matters of opinion, if they are sincere, are to be pitied, but not punished nor laughed at. The blindness of the understanding is as much to be pitied as the blindness of the eye; and there is neither jest nor guilt in a man's losing his way in either case. Charity bids us set him right if we can, by arguments and persuasions; but charity at the same time forbids either to punish or ridicule his misfortune. Every man's reason is, and must be, his guide; and I may as well expect that every man should be of my size and complexion as that he should reason just as I do. Every man seeks for truth; but God only knows who has found it. It is therefore as unjust to persecute as it is absurd to ridicule people for those several opinions which they cannot help entertaining upon the conviction of their reason. It is the man who tells or who acts a lie that is guilty, and not he who honestly and sincerely believes the lie. I really know nothing more criminal, more mean, and more ridiculous than lying. It is the production either of malice, cowardice, or vanity, and generally misses of its aim in every one of these views; for lies are always detected sooner or later. If I tell a malicious lie in order to affect any man's fortune or character, I may indeed injure him for some time, but I shall be sure to be the greatest sufferer myself at last; for as soon as ever I am detected (and detected I most certainly shall be), I am blasted for the infamous attempt, and whatever is said afterwards to the disadvantage of that person, however true, passes for calumny. If I lie or equivocate, for it is the same thing, in order to excuse myself for something that I have said or done, and to avoid the danger and the shame that I apprehend from it, I discover at once my fear as well as my falsehood, and only increase instead of avoiding the danger and the shame; I show myself to be the lowest and the meanest of mankind, and am sure to be always treated as such. Fear, instead of avoiding, invites danger, for concealed cowards will insult known ones. If one has had the misfortune to be in the wrong, there is something noble in frankly owning it; it is the only way of atoning for it, and the only way of being forgiven. Equivocating, evading, shuffling, in order to remove a present danger or inconveniency, is something so mean and betrays so much fear, that whoever practises them always deserves to be and often will be kicked. There is another sort of lies, inoffensive enough in themselves, but wonderfully ridiculous; I mean those lies which a mistaken vanity suggests, that defeat the very end for which they are calculated, and terminate in the humiliation and confusion of their author, who is sure to be detected. These are chiefly narrative and historical lies, all intended to do infinite honor to their author. He is always the hero of his own romances; he has been in dangers from which nobody but himself ever escaped; he has seen with his own eyes whatever other people have heard or read of; and has ridden more miles post in one day than ever courier went in two. He is soon discovered, and as soon becomes the object of universal contempt and ridicule. Remember then, as long as you live, that nothing but strict truth can carry you through the world with either your conscience or your honor unwounded. It is not only your duty, but your interest, — as a proof of which you may always observe that the greatest fools are the greatest liars. For my own part, I judge of every man's truth by his degree of understanding.

. . . .

XIV.

CAUTION IN FORMING FRIENDSHIPS. — GOOD COMPANY.

LONDON, *Oct.* 9, O. S. 1747.

DEAR BOY, — People of your age have, commonly, an unguarded frankness about them, which makes them the easy prey and bubbles [1] of the artful

---
[1] Dupes.

and the experienced; they look upon every knave or fool who tells them that he is their friend to be really so; and pay that profession of simulated friendship with an indiscreet and unbounded confidence, always to their loss, often to their ruin. Beware therefore, now that you are coming into the world, of these proffered friendships. Receive them with great civility but with great incredulity too, and pay them with compliments but not with confidence. Do not let your vanity and self-love make you suppose that people become your friends at first sight or even upon a short acquaintance. Real friendship is a slow grower, and never thrives unless ingrafted upon a stock of known and reciprocal merit.

There is another kind of nominal friendship among young people, which is warm for the time, but by good luck of short duration. This friendship is hastily produced by their being accidently thrown together and pursuing the same course of riot and debauchery. A fine friendship truly, and well cemented by drunkenness and lewdness! It should rather be called a conspiracy against morals and good manners, and be punished as such by the civil magistrate. However, they have the impudence and folly to call this confederacy a friendship. They lend one another money for bad purposes; they engage in quarrels, offensive and defensive, for their accomplices; they tell one another all they know, and often more too, when of a sudden some accident disperses them and they think no more of each other, unless it be to betray and laugh at their imprudent confidence. Remember to make a great difference between companions and friends; for a very complaisant and agreeable companion may, and often does, prove a very improper and a very dangerous friend. People will in a great degree, and not without reason, form their opinion of you upon that which they have of your friends; and there is a Spanish proverb which says very justly, "Tell me whom you live with and I will tell you who you are." One may fairly suppose that the man who makes a knave or a fool his friend has something very bad to do or to conceal. But at the same time that you carefully decline the friendship of knaves and fools, if it can be called friendship, there is no occasion to make either of them your enemies wantonly and unprovoked, for they are numerous bodies; and I would rather choose a secure neutrality than alliance or war with either of them. You may be a declared enemy to their vices and follies without being marked out by them as a personal one. Their enmity is the next dangerous thing to their friendship. Have a real reserve with almost everybody, and have a seeming reserve with almost nobody; for it is very disagreeable to seem reserved, and very dangerous not to be so. Few people find the true medium; many are ridiculously mysterious and reserved upon trifles, and many imprudently communicative of all they know.

The next thing to the choice of your friends is the choice of your company. Endeavor as much as you can to keep company with people above you; there you rise as much as you sink with people below you, for (as I have mentioned before) you are whatever the company you keep is. Do not mistake when I say company above you and think that I mean with regard to their birth, — that is the least consideration; but I mean with regard to their merit, and the light in which the world considers them.

There are two sorts of good company, — one which is called the *beau monde,* and consists of the people who have the lead in courts and in the gay part of life; the other consists of those who are distinguished by some peculiar merit, or who excel in some particular and valuable art or science. For my own part, I used to think myself in company as much above me, when I was with Mr. Addison and Mr. Pope,[1] as if I had been with all the princes in Europe. What I mean by low company — which should by all means be avoided — is the company of those who, absolutely insignificant and contemptible in themselves, think they are honored by being in your company, and who flatter every vice and every folly you have in order to engage you to converse with them. The pride of being the first of the company is but too common; but it is very silly and very prejudicial. Nothing in the world lets down a character quicker than that wrong turn.

---

[1] This allusion to Pope recalls Lord Chesterfield's epigram upon a full-length portrait of Beau Nash, placed in the Pump Room at Bath between the busts of Newton and Pope, —

> "This picture, placed the busts between,
> Gives satire all its strength;
> Wisdom and Wit are little seen,
> But Folly at full length."

You may possibly ask me whether a man has it always in his power to get the best company, and how? I say, Yes, he has, by deserving it; provided he is but in circumstances which enable him to appear upon the footing of a gentleman. Merit and good breeding will make their way everywhere. Knowledge will introduce him and good breeding will endear him to the best companies; for as I have often told you, politeness and good breeding are absolutely necessary to adorn any or all other good qualities or talents. Without them no knowledge, no perfection whatever, is seen in its best light. The scholar without good breeding is a pedant; the philosopher a cynic; the soldier a brute; and every man disagreeable.

I long to hear from my several correspondents at Leipzig of your arrival there, and what impression you make on them at first; for I have Arguses with a hundred eyes each who will watch you narrowly and relate to me faithfully. My accounts will certainly be true; it depends upon you entirely of what kind they shall be. Adieu.

XV.

THE ART OF PLEASING. — INDULGENCE FOR THE WEAKNESSES OF OTHERS.

LONDON, *Oct.* 16, O. S. 1747.

DEAR BOY, — The art of pleasing is a very necessary one to possess, but a very difficult one to acquire. It can hardly be reduced to rules; and your own good sense and observation will teach you more of it than I can. "Do as you would be done by" is the surest method that I know of pleasing. Observe carefully what pleases you in others, and probably the same thing in you will please others. If you are pleased with the complaisance and attention of others to your humors, your tastes, or your weaknesses, depend upon it the same complaisance and attention on your part to theirs will equally please them. Take the tone of the company that you are in, and do not pretend to give it; be serious, gay, or even trifling, as you find the present humor of the company, — this is an attention due from every individual to the majority. Do not tell stories in company; there is nothing more tedious and disagreeable. If by chance you know a very short story and exceedingly applicable to the present subject of conversation, tell it in as few words as possible; and even then throw out that you do not love to tell stories, but that the shortness of it tempted you. Of all things banish the egotism out of your conversation, and never think of entertaining people with your own personal concerns or private affairs. Though they are interesting to you, they are tedious and impertinent to everybody else; besides that, one cannot keep one's own private affairs too secret. Whatever you think your own excellencies may be, do not affectedly display them in company, nor labor, as many people do, to give that turn to the conversation which may supply you with an opportunity of exhibiting them. If they are real they will infallibly be discovered without your pointing them out yourself, and with much more advantage. Never maintain an argument with heat and clamor, though you think or know yourself to be in the right, but give your opinion modestly and coolly, which is the only way to convince; and if that does not do, try to change the conversation by saying, with good humor, "We shall hardly convince one another, nor is it necessary that we should; so let us talk of something else."

Remember that there is a local propriety to be observed in all companies, and that what is extremely proper in one company may be, and often is, highly improper in another.

The jokes, the *bon-mots*, the little adventures which may do very well in one company will seem flat and tedious when related in another. The particular characters, the habits, the cant of one company may give merit to a word or a gesture which would have none at all if divested of those accidental circumstances. Here people very commonly err; and fond of something that has entertained them in one company and in certain circumstances, repeat it with emphasis in another where it is either insipid, or, it may be, offensive by being ill-timed or misplaced. Nay, they often do it with this silly preamble, "I will tell you an excellent thing," or "I will tell you the best thing in the world." This raises expectations, which when absolutely disappointed, make the relator of this excellent thing look, very deservedly, like a fool.

If you would particularly gain the affection and friendship of particular people, whether men or women, endeavor to find out their predominant excellency, if they have one, and their prevailing weakness, which everybody has, and do justice to the one and something more than justice to the other. Men have various objects in which they may excel, or at least would be thought to excel; and though they love to hear justice done to them where they know that they excel, yet they are most and best flattered upon those points where they wish to excel and yet are doubtful whether they do or not. As, for example, Cardinal Richelieu, who was undoubtedly the ablest statesman of his time, or perhaps of any other, had the idle vanity of being thought the best poet, too; he envied the great Corneille his reputation, and ordered a criticism to be written upon the Cid. Those therefore who flattered skilfully said little to him of his abilities in state affairs, or at least but *en passant*, and as it might naturally occur. But the incense which they gave him the smoke of which they knew would turn his head in their favor, was as a *bel esprit* and a poet. Why? Because he was sure of one excellency, and distrustful as to the other. You will easily discover every man's prevailing vanity by observing his favorite topic of conversation; for every man talks most of what he has most a mind to be thought to excel in. Touch him but there, and you touch him to the quick. The late Sir Robert Walpole (who was certainly an able man) was little open to flattery upon that head, for he was in no doubt himself about it; but his prevailing weakness was to be thought to have a polite and happy turn to gallantry, of which he had undoubtedly less than any man living. It was his favorite and frequent subject of conversation, which proved to those who had any penetration that it was his prevailing weakness; and they applied to it with success.

Women have in general but one object, which is their beauty, upon which scarce any flattery is too gross for them to swallow. Nature has hardly formed a woman ugly enough to be insensible to flattery upon her person; if her face is so shocking that she must in some degree be conscious of it, her figure and her air, she trusts, make ample amends for it; if her figure is deformed, her face, she thinks, counterbalances it; if they are both bad, she comforts herself that she has graces, a certain manner, a *je ne sais quoi*[1] still more engaging than beauty. This truth is evident from the studied and elaborate dress of the ugliest women in the world. An undoubted, uncontested, conscious beauty is of all women the least sensible of flattery upon that head; she knows that it is her due, and is therefore obliged to nobody for giving it her. She must be flattered upon her understanding, which though she may possibly not doubt of herself, yet she suspects that men may distrust.

Do not mistake me and think that I mean to recommend to you abject and criminal flattery. No, flatter nobody's vices or crimes; on the contrary, abhor and discourage them. But there is no

[1] For an admirable analysis of this expression the reader is referred to the letter to his godson dated Aug. 9, 1768, and given in this volume at page 293.

living in the world without a complaisant indulgence for people's weaknesses and innocent though ridiculous vanities. If a man has a mind to be thought wiser and a woman handsomer than they really are, their error is a comfortable one to themselves and an innocent one with regard to other people; and I would rather make them my friends by indulging them in it than my enemies by endeavoring — and that to no purpose — to undeceive them.

There are little attentions likewise which are infinitely engaging, and which sensibly affect that degree of pride and self-love which is inseparable from human nature, as they are unquestionable proofs of the regard and consideration which we have for the person to whom we pay them. As, for example, to observe the little habits, the likings, the antipathies, and the tastes of those whom we would gain, and then take care to provide them with the one and to secure them from the other, — giving them genteelly to understand that you had observed that they liked such a dish or such a room, for which reason you had prepared it; or, on the contrary, that having observed they had an aversion to such a dish, a dislike to such a person, etc., you had taken care to avoid presenting them. Such attention to such trifles flatters self-love much more than greater things, as it makes people think themselves almost the only objects of your thoughts and care.

These are some of the *arcana* necessary for your initiation in the great society of the world. I wish I had known them better at your age; I have paid the price of three and fifty years for them, and shall not grudge it if you reap the advantage. Adieu.

XVI.

ON COMBINING STUDY WITH PLEASURE.

LONDON, *Oct.* 30, O. S. 1747.

. . . .
In short, be curious, attentive, inquisitive as to everything; listlessness and indolence are always blamable, but at your age they are unpardonable. Consider how precious and how important for all the rest of your life are your moments for these next three or four years, and do not lose one of them. Do not think I mean that you should study all day long; I am far from advising or desiring it; but I desire that you would be doing something or other all day long, and not neglect half hours and quarters of hours, which at the year's end amount to a great sum. For instance, there are many short intervals during the day between studies and pleasures; instead of sitting idle and yawning in those intervals, take up any book, though ever so trifling a one, even down to a jest-book, it is still better than doing nothing.

Nor do I call pleasures idleness or time lost, provided they are the pleasures of a rational being; on the contrary, a certain portion of your time employed in those pleasures is very usefully employed. Such are public spectacles, assemblies of good company, cheerful suppers, and even balls; but then these require attention, or else your time is quite lost.

There are a great many people who think themselves employed all day, and who if they were to cast up their accounts at night, would find that they had done just nothing. They have read two or three hours mechanically, without attending to what they read, and consequently without either retaining it or reasoning upon it. From thence they saunter into company, without taking any part in it, and without observing the characters of the persons or the subjects of the conversation; but are either thinking of some trifle, foreign to the present purpose, or often not thinking at all, — which silly and idle suspension of thought they would dignify with the name of *absence* and *distraction*. They go afterwards, it may be, to the play, where they gape at the company and the lights, but without minding the very thing they went to, — the play.

· · · · · · · · ·

XVII.

A WISE GUIDE THE BEST FRIEND.

LONDON, *Nov.* 24, 1747.

· · · · · · · · ·

Whatever your pleasures may be, I neither can nor shall envy you them, as old people are sometimes suspected by young people to do; and I shall only lament, if they should prove such as are unbecoming a man of honor or below a man of sense. But you will be the real sufferer if they are such. As therefore it is plain that I can have no other motive than that of affection in whatever I say to you, you ought to look upon me as your best, and for some years to come, your only friend.

True friendship requires certain proportions of age and manners, and can never subsist where they are extremely different, except in the relations of parent and child, where affection on one side and regard on the other make up the difference. The friendship which you may contract with people of your own age may be sincere, may be warm, but must be for some time reciprocally unprofitable, as there can be no experience on either side. The young leading the young is like the blind leading the blind,—"they will both fall into the ditch." The only sure guide is he who has often gone the road which you want to go. Let me be that guide, who have gone all roads, and who can consequently point out to you the best. If you ask me why I went any of the bad roads myself, I will answer you very truly that it was for want of a good guide; ill example invited me one way, and a good guide was wanting to show me a better. But if anybody capable of advising me had taken the same pains with me which I have taken, and will continue to take with you, I should have avoided many follies and inconveniences which undirected youth run me into. My father was neither desirous nor able to advise me;[1] which is what, I

---

[1] Lord Chesterfield's father seems to have contracted a dislike to him; and his early training fell to the care of his grandmother, Lady Halifax.

hope, you cannot say of yours. You see that I make use only of the word "advice," because I would much rather have the assent of your reason to my advice than the submission of your will to my authority. This, I persuade myself, will happen from that degree of sense which I think you have; and therefore I will go on advising, and with hopes of success.

. . . .

XVIII.

THE VALUE OF TIME.

LONDON, *Dec.* 11, O. S. 1747.

DEAR BOY, — There is nothing which I more wish that you should know, and which fewer people do know, than the true use and value of Time. It is in everybody's mouth, but in few people's practice. Every fool who slatterns away his whole time in nothings, utters, however, some trite commonplace sentence, of which there are millions, to prove at once the value and the fleetness of time. The sun-dials, likewise, all over Europe have some ingenious inscription to that effect; so that nobody squanders away their time without hearing and seeing daily how necessary it is to employ it well, and how irrecoverable it is if lost. But all these admonitions are useless where there is not a fund of good sense and reason to suggest them rather than receive them. By the manner in which you now tell me that you employ your time, I flatter myself that you have that fund; that is the fund which will make you rich indeed. I do not therefore mean to give you a critical essay upon the use and abuse of time, but I will only give you some hints with regard to the use of one particular period of that long time which, I hope, you have before you; I mean the next two years. Remember then, that whatever knowledge you do not solidly lay the foundation of before you are eighteen, you will never be the master of while you breathe. Knowledge is a comfortable and necessary retreat and shelter for us in an advanced age; and if we do not plant it while young, it will give us no shade when we grow old. I neither require nor expect from you great application to books after you are once thrown out into the great world. I know it is impossible, and it may even in some cases be improper; this therefore is your time, and your only time, for unwearied and uninterrupted application. If you should sometimes think it a little laborious, consider that labor is the unavoidable fatigue of a necessary journey. The more hours a day you travel, the sooner you will be at your journey's end. The sooner you are qualified for your liberty, the sooner you shall have it; and your manumission will entirely depend upon the manner in which you employ the intermediate time. I think I offer you a very good bargain when I promise you upon my word that if you will do everything that I would have you do till you are eighteen, I will do everything that you would have me do ever afterwards.

- . . . .

XIX.

TIME WELL AND TIME ILL SPENT.—OBSERVATION
RECOMMENDED.

BATH, *Feb.* 16, o. s. 1748.

DEAR BOY,—The first use that I made of my liberty[1] was to come hither, where I arrived yesterday. My health, though not fundamentally bad, yet for want of proper attention of late wanted some repairs, which these waters never fail giving it. I shall drink them a month, and return to London, there to enjoy the comforts of social life instead of groaning under the load of business. I have given the description of the life that I propose to lead for the future in this motto, which I have put up in the frieze of my library in my new house,[2]—

> Nunc veterum libris, nunc somno et, inertibus horis
> Ducere sollicitae jucunda oblivia vitae.

I must observe to you upon this occasion that the uninterrupted satisfaction which I expect to find in that library will be chiefly owing to my having employed some part of my life well at your age. I wish I had employed it better, and my satisfaction would now be complete; but, however, I planted while young that degree of knowledge which is now my refuge and my shelter. Make your plantations still more extensive; they will more than pay you for your trouble. I do not regret the time that I passed

---

[1] He had just resigned the office of Secretary of State.
[2] Chesterfield House in London.

in pleasures; they were seasonable; they were the pleasures of youth, and I enjoyed them while young. If I had not, I should probably have overvalued them now, as we are very apt to do what we do not know; but knowing them as I do, I know their real value, and how much they are generally overrated. Nor do I regret the time that I have passed in business for the same reason; those who see only the outside of it imagine it has hidden charms, which they pant after, and nothing but acquaintance can undeceive them. I, who have been behind the scenes both of pleasure and business, and have seen all the springs and pulleys of those decorations which astonish and dazzle the audience, retire not only without regret but with contentment and satisfaction. But what I do and ever shall regret, is the time which, while young, I lost in mere idleness, and in doing nothing. This is the common effect of the inconsideracy of youth, against which I beg you will be most carefully upon your guard. The value of moments when cast up is immense, if well employed; if thrown away, their loss is irrecoverable. Every moment may be put to some use, and that with much more pleasure than if unemployed. Do not imagine that by the employment of time I mean an uninterrupted application to serious studies. No; pleasures are at proper times both as necessary and as useful; they fashion and form you for the world; they teach you characters, and show you the human heart in its unguarded minutes. But then remember to make that use of them. I have known many people from laziness of mind go through both pleasure and business with equal inattention, neither enjoying the one nor doing the other; thinking themselves men of pleasure because they were mingled with those who were, and men of business because they had business to do, though they did not do it. Whatever you do, do it to the purpose; do it thoroughly, not superficially. *Approfondissez:* go to the bottom of things. Anything half done or half known is, in my mind, neither done nor known at all. Nay, worse, for it often misleads. There is hardly any place or any company where you may not gain knowledge, if you please; almost everybody knows some one thing, and is glad to talk upon that one thing. Seek and you will find, in this world as well as in the next. See everything, inquire into everything; and you may excuse your curiosity and the questions you ask, which otherwise might be thought impertinent, by your manner of asking them,— for most things depend a great deal upon the manner: as for example, "I am afraid that I am very troublesome with my questions, but nobody can inform me so well as you," or something of that kind.

Now that you are in a Lutheran country, go to their churches and observe the manner of their public worship; attend to their ceremonies and inquire the meaning and intention of every one of them. And as you will soon understand German well enough, attend to their sermons and observe their manner of preaching. Inform yourself of their church government, whether it resides in the sovereign or in consistories and synods; whence arises the maintenance of their clergy, whether from tithes as in England, or from voluntary contributions or from pensions from the State. Do the same thing when you are in Roman-Catholic countries; go to their churches, see all their ceremonies, ask the meaning of them, get the terms explained to you, — as, for instance, Prime, Tierce, Sexte, Nones, Matins, Angelus, High Mass, Vespers, Complies, etc. Inform yourself of their several religious orders, their founders, their rules, their vows, their habits, their revenues, etc. But when you frequent places of public worship, as I would have you go to all the different ones you meet with, remember that however erroneous, they are none of them objects of laughter and ridicule. Honest error is to be pitied, not ridiculed. The object of all the public worships in the world is the same, — it is that great eternal Being who created everything. The different manners of worship are by no means subjects of ridicule. Each sect thinks its own is the best, and I know no infallible judge in this world to decide which is the best. Make the same inquiries, wherever you are, concerning the revenues, the military establishment, the trade, the commerce, and the police of every country. And you would do well to keep a blank-paper book, which the Germans call an *album;* and there, instead of desiring, as they do, every fool they meet with to scribble something, write down all these things as soon as they come to your knowledge from good authorities.

. . . .

XX.

RIGHT USE OF LEARNING: ABSURDITIES OF PEDANTRY.

BATH, *Feb.* 22, O. S. 1748.

DEAR BOY, — Every excellency, and every virtue, has its kindred vice or weakness, and if carried beyond certain bounds sinks into one or the other. Generosity often runs into profusion, economy into avarice, courage into rashness, caution into timidity, and so on, insomuch that I believe there is more judgment required for the proper conduct of our virtues than for avoiding their opposite vices. Vice in its true light is so deformed that it shocks us at first sight, and would hardly ever seduce us, if it did not at first wear the mask of some virtue. But virtue is in itself so beautiful, that it charms us at first sight; engages us more and more upon further acquaintance; and as with other beauties, we think excess impossible. It is here that judgment is necessary to moderate and direct the effects of an excellent cause. I shall apply this reasoning at present not to any particular virtue, but to an excellency, which for want of judgment is often the cause of ridiculous and blamable effects; I mean great learning, — which if not accompanied with sound judgment, frequently carries us into error, pride, and pedantry. As I hope you will possess that excellency in its utmost extent and yet without its too common failings, the hints which my experience can suggest may probably not be useless to you.

Some learned men, proud of their knowledge, only speak to decide, and give judgment without appeal; the consequence of which is that mankind, provoked by the insult and injured by the oppression, revolt, and in order to shake off the tyranny, even call the lawful authority in question. The more you know the modester you should be; and (by the by) that modesty is the surest way of gratifying your vanity. Even where you are sure, seem rather doubtful; represent but do not pronounce; and if you would convince others, seem open to conviction yourself.

Others, to show their learning, or often from the prejudices of a school-education, where they hear of nothing else, are always talking of the Ancients as something more than men and of the Moderns as something less. They are never without a classic or two in their pockets; they stick to the old good sense; they read none of the modern trash; and will show you plainly that no improvement has been made in any one art or science these last seventeen hundred years. I would by no means have you disown your acquaintance with the ancients, but still less would I have you brag of an exclusive intimacy with them. Speak of the moderns without contempt and of the ancients without idolatry; judge them all by their merits, but not by their ages; and if you happen to have an Elzevir classic in your pocket, neither show it nor mention it.

Some great scholars most absurdly draw all their maxims, both for public and private life, from what they call parallel cases in the ancient authors, without considering that in the first place there never were, since the creation of the world, two cases exactly parallel; and in the next place that there never was a case stated or even known by any historian with every one of its circumstances, which however ought to be known in order to be reasoned from. Reason upon the case itself and the several circumstances that attend it, and act accordingly, but not from the authority of ancient poets or historians. Take into your consideration, if you please, cases seemingly analogous; but take them as helps only, not as guides. We are really so prejudiced by our education, that, as the ancients deified their heroes, we deify their madmen, — of which, with all due regard for antiquity, I take Leonidas and Curtius to have been two distinguished ones. And yet a solid pedant would, in a speech in Parliament relative to a tax of two-pence in the pound upon some commodity or other, quote those two heroes as examples of what we ought to do and suffer for our country. I have known these absurdities carried so far by people of injudicious learning that I should not be surprised if some of them were to propose, while we are at war with the Gauls, that a number of geese should be kept in the Tower, upon account of the infinite advantage which Rome received *in a parallel case* from a certain number of geese in the Capitol. This way of reasoning and this way of speaking will always form a poor politician and a puerile declaimer.

There is another species of learned men, who though less dogmatical and supercilious, are not less impertinent. These are the communicative and shining pedants who adorn their conversation, even with women, by happy quotations of Greek and Latin, and who have contracted such a familiarity with the Greek and Roman authors that they call them by certain names or epithets denoting intimacy, — as *old* Homer; that *sly rogue* Horace; *Maro*, instead of Virgil; and *Naso*, instead of Ovid. These are often imitated by coxcombs who have no learning at all, but who have got some names and some scraps of ancient authors by heart, which they improperly and impertinently retail in all companies, in hopes of passing for scholars. If therefore you would avoid the accusation of pedantry on one hand, or the suspicion of ignorance on the other, abstain from learned ostentation. Speak the language of the company that you are in; speak it purely, and unlarded with any other. Never seem wiser nor more learned than the people you are with. Wear your learning, like your watch, in a private pocket, and do not pull it out and strike it merely to show that you have one. If you are asked what o'clock it is, tell it, but do not proclaim it hourly and unasked, like the watchman.

. . . .

XXI.

THE GRACES. — THE ABSURDITY OF LAUGHTER.

BATH, *March* 9, O. S. 1748.

DEAR BOY, — I must from time to time remind you of what I have often recommended to you, and of what you cannot attend to too much, — *Sacrifice to the Graces*. The different effects of the same things said or done when accompanied or abandoned by them, is almost inconceivable. They prepare the way to the heart; and the heart has such an influence over the understanding, that it is worth while to engage it in our interest. It is the whole of women, who are guided by nothing else; and it has so much to say even with men, and the ablest men too, that it commonly triumphs in every struggle with the understanding. Monsieur de Rochefoucault, in his Maxims, says that "l'esprit est souvent la dupe du cœur." If he had said, instead of *souvent*, *presque toujours*, I fear he would have been nearer the truth. This being the case, aim at the heart. Intrinsic merit alone will not do. It will gain you the general esteem of all, but not the particular affection, that is, the heart, of any. To engage the affection of any particular person, you must, over and above your general merit, have some particular merit to that person by services done or offered, by expressions of regard and esteem, by complaisance, attentions, etc., for him; and the graceful manner of doing all these things opens the way to the heart, and facilitates or rather insures their effects. From your own observation, reflect what a disagreeable impression an awkward address, a slovenly figure, an ungraceful manner of speaking, — whether stuttering, muttering, monotony, or drawling, — an unattentive behavior, etc., make upon you, at first sight, in a stranger, and how they prejudice you against him, though for aught you know he may have great intrinsic sense and merit. And reflect on the other hand how much the opposites of all these things prepossess you at first sight in favor of those who enjoy them. You wish to find all good qualities in them, and are in some degree disappointed if you do not. A thousand little things, not separately to be defined, conspire to form these graces, this *je ne sais quoi*, that always pleases. A pretty person, genteel motions, a proper degree of dress, an harmonious voice, something open and cheerful in the countenance but without laughing, a distinct and properly varied manner of speaking, — all these things, and many others, are necessary ingredients in the composition of the pleasing *je ne sais quoi*, which everybody feels though nobody can describe. Observe carefully, then, what displeases or pleases you in others, and be persuaded that in general the same things will please or displease them in you. Having mentioned laughing, I must particularly warn you against it; and I could heartily wish that you may often be seen to smile but never heard to laugh while you live. Frequent and loud laughter is the characteristic of folly and ill manners; it is the manner in which the mob express their silly joy at silly things; and they call it being merry. In my mind, there is nothing so illiberal and so ill bred as audible laughter. True wit or sense never yet made anybody laugh; they are above it; they please the mind, and give a cheerfulness to the countenance. But it is low buffoonery or silly accidents that always excite laughter; and that is what people of sense and breeding should show themselves above. A man's going to sit down in the supposition that he has a chair behind him, and falling down for want of one, sets a whole company a-laughing, when all the wit in the world would not do it, — a plain proof in my mind how low and unbecoming a thing laughter is, not to mention the disagreeable noise that it makes, and the shocking distortion of the face that it occasions. Laughter is easily restrained by a very little reflection; but as it is generally connected with the idea of gayety, people do not enough attend to its absurdity. I am neither of a melancholy nor a cynical disposition, and am as willing and as apt to be pleased as anybody; but I am sure that since I have had the full use of my reason, nobody has ever heard me laugh. Many people, at first from awkwardness and *mauvaise honte*, have got a very disagreeable and silly trick of laughing whenever they speak; and I know a man of very good parts, Mr. Waller, who cannot say the commonest thing without laughing, which makes those who do not know him take him at first for a natural fool. This and many other very disagreeable habits are owing to *mauvaise honte* at their first setting out in the world. They are ashamed in company, and so disconcerted that they do not know what they do, and try a thousand tricks to keep themselves in countenance, which tricks afterwards grow habitual to them. Some scratch their heads, others twirl their hats; in short, every awkward, ill-bred body has his trick. But the frequency does not justify the thing, and all these vulgar habits and awkwardnesses, though not criminal, indeed, are most carefully to be guarded against, as they are great bars in the way of the art of pleasing. Remember that to please is almost to prevail, or at least a necessary previous step to it.

. . . .

XXII.

DISSIMULATION FOUND NOT ONLY IN COURTS.— TRITE OBSERVATIONS.

LONDON, *May* 10, 1748.

. . . .

It is a trite and commonplace observation that Courts are the seat of falsehood and dissimulation. That, like many, I might say most, commonplace observations, is false. Falsehood and dissimulation are certainly to be found at courts; but where are they not to be found? Cottages have them as well as courts, only with worse manners. A couple of neighboring farmers in a village will contrive and practise as many tricks to overreach each other at the next market, or to supplant each other in the favor of the squire, as any two courtiers can do to supplant each other in the favor of their prince. Whatever poets may write, or fools believe, of rural innocence and truth and of the perfidy of courts, this is most undoubtedly true, — that shepherds and ministers are both men, their nature and passions the same, the modes of them only different.

Having mentioned commonplace observations, I will particularly caution you against either using, believing, or approving them. They are the common topics of witlings and coxcombs; those who really have wit have the utmost contempt for them, and scorn even to laugh at the pert things that those would-be wits say upon such subjects.

Religion is one of their favorite topics. It is all priestcraft, and an invention contrived and carried on by priests of all religions for their own power and profit. From this absurd and false principle flow the commonplace insipid jokes and insults upon the clergy. With these people, every priest, of every religion, is either a public or a concealed unbeliever, drunkard, and rake; whereas I conceive that priests are extremely like other men, and neither the better nor the worse for wearing a gown or a surplice; but if they are different from other people, probably it is rather on the side of religion and morality, or at least decency, from their education and manner of life.

Another common topic for false wit and cold raillery is matrimony. Every man and his wife hate each other cordially, whatever they may pretend in public to the contrary. The husband certainly wishes his wife at the devil, and the wife certainly deceives her husband; whereas I presume that men and their wives neither love nor hate each other the more upon account of the form of matrimony which has been said over them.

. . . .

These, and many other commonplace reflections upon nations, or professions in general,— which are at least as often false as true,— are the poor refuge of people who have neither wit nor invention of their own, but endeavor to shine in company by second-hand finery. I always put these pert jackanapeses out of countenance by looking extremely grave when they expect that I should laugh at their pleasantries; and by saying *well*, and *so*, as if they had not done, and that the sting were still to come. This disconcerts them, as they have no resources in themselves and have but one set of jokes to live upon.

. . . .

XXIII.

AN AWKWARD MAN AT COURT. — WELL-BRED EASE.

LONDON, *May* 17, O. S. 1748.

DEAR BOY, — I received yesterday your letter of the 16th, N. S., and have in consequence of it written this day to Sir Charles Williams to thank him for all the civilities he has shown you. Your first setting out at court has, I find, been very favorable, and his Polish Majesty has distinguished you. I hope you received that mark of distinction with respect and with steadiness, which is the proper behavior of a man of fashion. People of a low, obscure education cannot stand the rays of greatness; they are frightened out of their wits when kings and great men speak to them; they are awkward, ashamed, and do not know what or how to answer; whereas, *les honnêtes gens* are not dazzled by superior rank; they know and pay all the respect that is due to it; but they do it without being disconcerted, and can converse just as easily with a king as with any one of his subjects. That is the great advantage of being introduced young into good company, and being used early to converse with one's superiors. How many men have I seen here, who, after having had the full benefit of an English education, first at school and then at the university, when they have been presented to the king did not know whether they stood upon their heads or their heels! If the king spoke to them, they were annihilated; they trembled, endeavored to put their hands in their pockets, and missed them; let their hats fall and were ashamed to take them up; and in short, put themselves in every attitude but the right, that is, the easy and natural one. The characteristic of a well-bred man is to converse with his inferiors without insolence, and with his superiors with respect and ease. He talks to kings without concern; he trifles with women of the first condition with familiarity, gayety, but respect; and converses with his equals whether he is acquainted with them or not, upon general common topics that are not however quite frivolous, without the least concern of mind or awkwardness of body, neither of which can appear to advantage but when they are perfectly easy.

. . . .

XXIV.

THE LAZY MIND AND THE FRIVOLOUS MIND.

LONDON, *July* 26, O. S. 1748.

DEAR BOY, — There are two sorts of understandings, one of which hinders a man from ever being considerable, and the other commonly makes him ridiculous, — I mean the lazy mind and the trifling, frivolous mind. Yours I hope is neither. The lazy mind will not take the trouble of going to the bottom of anything, but discouraged by the first difficulties (and everything worth knowing or having is attained with some), stops short, contents itself with easy and consequently superficial knowledge, and prefers a great degree of ignorance to a small degree of trouble. These people either think or represent most things as impossible, whereas few things are so to industry and activity. But difficulties seem to them impossibilities, or at least they pretend to think them so by way of excuse for their laziness. An hour's attention to the same subject is too laborious for them; they take everything in the light in which it first presents itself, never consider it in all its different views, and in short never think it thorough. The consequence of this is that when they come to speak upon these subjects before people who have considered them with attention, they only discover their own ignorance and laziness, and lay themselves open to answers that put them in confusion. Do not then be discouraged by the first difficulties, but *contra audentior ito;* and resolve to go to the bottom of all those things which every gentleman ought to know well. Those arts or sciences which are peculiar to certain professions need not be deeply known by those who are not intended for those professions; as, for instance, fortification and navigation; of both which, a superficial and general knowledge such as the common course of conversation with a very little inquiry on your part will give you, is sufficient. Though, by the way, a little more knowledge of fortification may be of some use to you, as the events of war in sieges make many of the terms of that science occur frequently in common conversation; and one would be sorry to say, like the Marquis de Mascarille in Molière's "Précieuses Ridicules," when he hears of *une demie lune*, " Ma foi ! c'étoit bien une lune toute entière." But those things which every gentleman, independently of profession, should know, he ought to know well, and dive into all the depth of them. Such are languages, history, and geography, ancient and modern, philosophy, rational logic, rhetoric; and for you particularly, the constitutions, and the civil and military state of every country in Europe. This, I confess, is a pretty large circle of knowledge, attended with some difficulties, and requiring some trouble; which, however, an active and industrious mind will overcome, and be amply repaid. The trifling and frivolous mind is always busied, but to little purpose; it takes little objects for great ones, and throws away upon trifles that time and attention which only important things deserve. Knickknacks, butterflies, shells, insects, etc., are the subjects of their most serious researches. They contemplate the dress, not the characters, of the company they keep. They attend more to the decorations of a play than to the sense of it, and to the ceremonies of a court more than to its politics. Such an employment of time is an absolute loss of it. You have now, at most, three years to employ, either well or ill; for as I have often told you, you will be all your life what you shall be three years hence. For God's sake then reflect. Will you throw this time away either in laziness or in trifles; or will you not rather employ every moment of it in a manner that must so soon reward you with so much pleasure, figure, and character? I cannot, I will not, doubt of your choice. Read only useful books; and never quit a subject till you are thoroughly master of it, but read and inquire on till then. When you are in company, bring the conversation to some useful subject, but *à portée* of that company. Points of history, matters of literature, the customs of particular countries, the several orders of knighthood, as Teutonic, Maltese, etc., are surely better subjects of conversation than the weather, dress, or fiddle-faddle stories that carry no information along with them. The characters of kings and great men are only to be learned in conversation; for they are never fairly written during their lives. This therefore is an entertaining and instructive subject of conversation, and will likewise give you an opportunity of observing how very differently characters are given from the different passions and views of those who give them. Never be ashamed nor afraid of asking questions; for if they lead to information, and if you accompany them with some excuse, you will never be reckoned an impertinent or rude questioner. All those things, in the common course of life, depend entirely upon the manner; and in that respect the vulgar saying is true, "That one man can better steal a horse than another look over the hedge." There are few things that may not be said in some manner or other; either in a seeming confidence, or a genteel irony, or introduced with wit; and one great part of the knowledge of the world consists in knowing when and where to make use of these different manners. The graces of the person, the countenance, and the way of speaking contribute so much to this, that I am convinced the very same thing said by a genteel person in an engaging way, and *gracefully* and *distinctly* spoken, would please, which would shock, if *muttered* out by an awkward figure with a sullen, serious countenance. The poets always represent Venus as attended by the three Graces, to intimate that even beauty will not do without. I think they should have given Minerva three also, for without them I am sure learning is very unattractive. Invoke them then, *distinctly*, to accompany all your words and motions. Adieu.

XXV.

HOW HISTORY SHOULD BE READ.

LONDON, *Aug.* 30, O. S. 1748.

DEAR BOY, — Your reflections upon the conduct of France from the treaty of Münster to this time are very just; and I am very glad to find by them, that you not only read, but that you think and reflect upon what you read. Many great readers load their memories without exercising their judgments, and make lumber-rooms of their heads instead of furnishing them usefully; facts are heaped upon facts without order or distinction, and may justly be said to compose that

" ———Rudis indigestaque moles
   Quam dixere chaos."

Go on, then, in the way of reading that you are in; take nothing for granted upon the bare authority of the author, but weigh and consider in your own mind the probability of the facts and the justness of the reflections. Consult different authors upon the same facts, and form your opinion upon the greater or lesser degree of probability arising from the whole, — which in my mind is the utmost stretch of historical faith, certainty (I fear) not being to be found. When a historian pretends to give you the causes and motives of events, compare those causes and motives with the characters and interests of the parties concerned, and judge for yourself whether they correspond or not. Consider whether you cannot assign others more probable; and in that examination do not despise some very mean and trifling causes of the actions of great men; for so various and inconsistent is human nature, so strong and so changeable are our passions, so fluctuating are our wills, and so much are our minds influenced by the accidents of our bodies, that every man is more the man of the day than a regular consequential character. The best have something bad, and something little; the worst have something good, and sometimes something great, — for I do not believe what Velleius Paterculus (for the sake of saying a pretty thing) says of Scipio, " Qui nihil non laudandum aut fecit, aut dixit, aut sensit." As for the reflections of historians with which they think it necessary to interlard their histories or at least to conclude their chapters, — and which in the French histories are always introduced with a *tant il est vrai*, and in the English, *so true it is*, — do not adopt them implicitly upon the credit of the author, but analyze them yourself, and judge whether they are true or not.

. . . .

XXVI.

GENERAL CHARACTER OF WOMEN. — RIGHT USE OF WIT.

LONDON, *Sept.* 5, O. S. 1748.

. . . .

As women are a considerable or at least a pretty numerous part of company, and as their suffrages go a great way towards establishing a man's character in the fashionable part of the world,—which is of great importance to the fortune and figure he proposes to make in it,—it is necessary to please them. I will therefore upon this subject let you into certain *arcana*, that will be very useful for you to know, but which you must with the utmost care conceal, and never seem to know. Women then are only children of a larger growth; they have an entertaining tattle and sometimes wit, but for solid, reasoning good-sense, I never knew in my life one that had it, or who reasoned or acted consequentially for four-and-twenty hours together. Some little passion or humor always breaks in upon their best resolutions. Their beauty neglected or controverted, their age increased, or their supposed understandings depreciated instantly kindles their little passions, and overturns any system of consequential conduct that in their most reasonable moments they might have been capable of forming. A man of sense only trifles with them, plays with them, humors and flatters them, as he does with a sprightly, forward child; but he neither consults them about nor trusts them with serious matters, though he often makes them believe that he does both, which is the thing in the world that they are proud of; for they love mightily to be dabbling in business,—which, by the way, they always spoil,— and being justly distrustful that men in general look upon them in a trifling light, they almost adore that man who talks more seriously to them, and who seems to consult and trust them : I say, who seems;

for weak men really do, but wise ones only seem to do it. No flattery is either too high or too low for them; they will greedily swallow the highest and gratefully accept of the lowest; and you may safely flatter any woman from her understanding down to the exquisite taste of her fan. Women who are either indisputably beautiful or indisputably ugly are best flattered upon the score of their understandings; but those who are in a state of mediocrity are best flattered upon their beauty, or at least their graces, for every woman who is not absolutely ugly thinks herself handsome; but not hearing often that she is so is the more grateful and the more obliged to the few who tell her so; whereas a decided and conscious beauty looks upon every tribute paid to her beauty only as her due, but wants to shine and to be considered on the side of her understanding; and a woman who is ugly enough to know that she is so, knows that she has nothing left for it but her understanding, which is consequently — and probably in more senses than one — her weak side. But these are secrets which you must keep inviolably, if you would not like Orpheus be torn to pieces by the whole sex; on the contrary, a man who thinks of living in the great world must be gallant, polite, and attentive to please the women. They have from the weakness of men more or less influence in all courts; they absolutely stamp every man's character in the *beau monde* and make it either current, or cry it down and stop it in payments. It is therefore absolutely necessary to manage, please, and flatter them, and never to discover the least marks of contempt, which is what they never forgive; but in this they are not singular, for it is the same with men, who will much sooner forgive an injustice than an insult. Every man is not ambitious, or courteous, or passionate; but every man has pride enough in his composition to feel and resent the least slight and contempt. Remember therefore most carefully to conceal your contempt, however just, wherever you would not make an implacable enemy. Men are much more unwilling to have their weaknesses and their imperfections known than their crimes; and if you hint to a man that you think him silly, ignorant, or even ill bred or awkward, he will hate you more and longer than if you tell him plainly that you think him a rogue. Never yield to that temptation, which to most young men is very strong, of exposing other people's weaknesses and infirmities for the sake either of diverting the company or showing your own superiority. You may get the laugh on your side by it for the present, but you will make enemies by it forever; and even those who laugh with you then will upon reflection fear, and consequently hate you; besides that, it is ill-natured, and a good heart desires rather to conceal than expose other people's weaknesses or misfortunes. If you have wit, use it to please and not to hurt; you may shine like the sun in the temperate zones without scorching. Here it is wished for; under the line it is dreaded.

These are some of the hints which my long experience in the great world enables me to give you, and which if you attend to them may prove useful to you in your journey through it. I wish it may be a prosperous one; at least I am sure that it must be your own fault if it is not.

. . . .

XXVII.

OUR TENDENCY TO EXALT THE PAST. — ON SECRETS.

LONDON, *Sept.* 13, O. S. 1748.

. . . .

Another very just observation of the Cardinal's[1] is, that the things which happen in our own times and which we see ourselves do not surprise us near so much as the things which we read of in times past, though not in the least more extraordinary; and adds that he is persuaded that when Caligula made his horse a consul, the people of Rome at that time were not greatly surprised at it, having necessarily been in some degree prepared for it by an insensible gradation of extravagances from the same quarter. This is so true, that we read every day with astonishment things which we see every day without surprise. We wonder at the intrepidity of a Leonidas, a Codrus, and a Curtius; and are not the least surprised to hear of a sea-captain who has blown up his ship, his crew, and himself, that they might not fall into the hands of the enemies of his country. I cannot help reading of Porsenna and Regulus with surprise and reverence; and yet I remember that I saw without

[1] The Cardinal De Retz.

either the execution of Shepherd,[1] a boy of eighteen years old, who intended to shoot the late king, and who would have been pardoned if he would have expressed the least sorrow for his intended crime; but on the contrary he declared that if he was pardoned he would attempt it again; that he thought it a duty which he owed to his country; and that he died with pleasure for having endeavored to perform it. Reason equals Shepherd to Regulus; but prejudice and the recency of the fact make Shepherd a common malefactor and Regulus a hero.

. . . .

The last observation that I shall now mention of the Cardinal's is "That a secret is more easily kept by a good many people than one commonly imagines." By this he means a secret of importance among people interested in the keeping of it; and it is certain that people of business know the importance of secrecy, and will observe it where they are concerned in the event. To go and tell any friend, wife, or mistress any secret with which they have nothing to do, is discovering to them such an unretentive weakness as must convince them that you will tell it to twenty others, and consequently that they may reveal it without the risk of being discovered. But a secret properly communicated only to those who are to be concerned in the thing in question will probably be kept by them, though they

---

[1] James Shepherd, a coach-painter's apprentice, was executed at Tyburn for high treason, March 17, 1718, in the reign of George the First.

should be a good many. Little secrets are commonly told again, but great ones are generally kept. Adieu!

XXVIII.

AGAINST THE REFINEMENTS OF CASUISTRY.

LONDON, *Sept.* 27, O. S. 1748.

. . . .

Pray let no quibbles of lawyers, no refinements of casuists, break into the plain notions of right and wrong which every man's right reason and plain common-sense suggest to him. To do as you would be done by is the plain, sure, and undisputed rule of morality and justice. Stick to that; and be convinced that whatever breaks into it in any degree, however speciously it may be turned, and however puzzling it may be to answer it, is notwithstanding false in itself, unjust, and criminal. I do not know a crime in the world which is not by the casuists among the Jesuits (especially the twenty-four collected, I think, by Escobar) allowed in some or many cases not to be criminal. The principles first laid down by them are often specious, the reasonings plausible, but the conclusion always a lie; for it is contrary to that evident and undeniable rule of justice which I have mentioned above, of not doing to any one what you would not have him do to you. But, however, these refined pieces of casuistry and sophistry being very convenient and welcome to people's passions and appetites, they gladly accept the indulgence without desiring to detect the fallacy of the reasoning: and indeed many, I might say most people, are not able to do it, — which makes the publication of such quibblings and refinements the more pernicious. I am no skilful casuist nor subtle disputant; and yet I would undertake to justify and qualify the profession of a highwayman, step by step, and so plausibly as to make many ignorant people embrace the profession as an innocent if not even a laudable one, and to puzzle people of some degree of knowledge to answer me point by point. I have seen a book, entitled "Quidlibet ex Quolibet," or the art of making anything out of anything; which is not so difficult as it would seem, if once one quits certain plain truths, obvious in gross to every understanding, in order to run after the ingenious refinements of warm imaginations and speculative reasonings. Doctor Berkeley, Bishop of Cloyne, a very worthy, ingenious, and learned man, has written a book to prove that there is no such thing as matter, and that nothing exists but in idea; that you and I only fancy ourselves eating, drinking, and sleeping, you at Leipsic, and I at London; that we think we have flesh and blood, legs, arms, etc., but that we are only spirit. His arguments are strictly speaking unanswerable; but yet I am so far from being convinced by them that I am determined to go on to eat and drink, and walk and ride, in order to keep that *matter*, which I so mistakenly imagine my body at present to consist of, in as good plight as possible. Common-sense (which in truth is very uncommon) is the best sense I know of. Abide by it;

it will counsel you best. Read and hear for your amusement ingenious systems, nice questions subtilely agitated, with all the refinements that warm imaginations suggest; but consider them only as exercitations for the mind, and return always to settle with common-sense.

. . . .

XXIX.

TRUE GOOD COMPANY DEFINED.

October 12, o. s. 1748.

. . . .

To keep good company, especially at your first setting out, is the way to receive good impressions. If you ask me what I mean by good company, I will confess to you that it is pretty difficult to define; but I will endeavor to make you understand it as well as I can.

Good company is not what respective sets of company are pleased either to call or think themselves, but it is that company which all the people of the place call, and acknowledge to be, good company, notwithstanding some objections which they may form to some of the individuals who compose it. It consists chiefly (but by no means without exception) of people of considerable birth, rank, and character; for people of neither birth nor rank are frequently and very justly admitted into it, if distinguished by any peculiar merit, or eminency in any liberal art or science. Nay, so motley a thing is good company that many people without birth, rank, or merit intrude into it by their own forwardness, and others slide into it by the protection of some considerable person; and some even of indifferent characters and morals make part of it. But in the main, the good part preponderates, and people of infamous and blasted characters are never admitted. In this fashionable good company, the best manners and the best language of the place are most unquestionably to be learnt; for they establish and give the tone to both, which are therefore called the language and manners of good company, there being no legal tribunal to ascertain either.

A company consisting wholly of people of the first quality cannot for that reason be called good company, in the common acceptation of the phrase, unless they are into the bargain the fashionable and accredited company of the place; for people of the very first quality can be as silly, as ill bred, and as worthless as people of the meanest degree. On the other hand, a company consisting entirely of people of very low condition, whatever their merit or parts may be, can never be called good company; and consequently should not be much frequented, though by no means despised.

A company wholly composed of men of learning, though greatly to be valued and respected, is not meant by the words " good company;" they cannot have the easy manners and *tournure* of the world, as they do not live in it. If you can bear your part well in such a company, it is extremely right to be in it sometimes, and you will be but more esteemed in other companies for having a place in that. But then do not let it engross you; for if you do, you will be only considered as one of the *literati* by profession, which is not the way either to shine or rise in the world.

The company of professed wits and poets is extremely inviting to most young men, who if they have wit themselves, are pleased with it, and if they have none, are sillily proud of being one of it; but it should be frequented with moderation and judgment, and you should by no means give yourself up to it. A wit is a very unpopular denomination, as it carries terror along with it; and people in general are as much afraid of a live wit in company as a woman is of a gun, which she thinks may go off of itself and do her a mischief. Their acquaintance is however worth seeking, and their company worth frequenting; but not exclusively of others, nor to such a degree as to be considered only as one of that particular set.

But the company which of all others you should most carefully avoid is that low company which in every sense of the word is low indeed,—low in rank, low in parts, low in manners, and low in merit. You will perhaps be surprised that I should think it necessary to warn you against such company, but yet I do not think it wholly unnecessary from the many instances which I have seen of men of sense and rank discredited, vilified, and undone by keeping such company. Vanity, that source of many of our follies and of some of our crimes, has sunk many a man into company in every light infinitely below himself, for the sake of being the first man in it. There he dictates, is applauded, admired; and for the sake of being the *Coryphæus* of that wretched chorus, disgraces and disqualifies himself soon for any better company. Depend upon it, you will sink or rise to the level of the company which you commonly keep; people will judge of you, and not unreasonably, by that. There is good sense in the Spanish saying, "Tell me whom you live with, and I will tell you who you are." Make it therefore your business, wherever you are, to get into that company which everybody in the place allows to be the best company next to their own; which is the best definition that I can give you of good company. But here, too, one caution is very necessary, for want of which many young men have been ruined, even in good company. Good company (as I have before observed) is composed of a great variety of fashionable people, whose characters and morals are very different, though their manners are pretty much the same. When a young man, new in the world, first gets into that company, he very rightly determines to conform to and imitate it. But then he too often and fatally mistakes the objects of his imitation. He has often heard that absurd term of "genteel and fashionable vices." He there sees some people who shine and who in general are admired and esteemed, and observes that these people are . . . drunkards or gamesters, upon which he adopts their vices, mistaking their defects for their perfections, and thinking that they owe their fashion and their lustre to those genteel vices. Whereas it is exactly the reverse; for these people have acquired their reputation by their parts, their learning, their good breeding, and other accomplishments, and are only blemished and lowered, in the opinions of all reasonable people, and of their own in time, by these genteel and fashionable vices.

. . . .

XXX.

CONDUCT IN GOOD COMPANY.—ON MIMICRY.

BATH, *Oct.* 19, O. S. 1748.

DEAR BOY,—Having in my last pointed out what sort of company you should keep, I will now give you some rules for your conduct in it,—rules which my own experience and observation enable me to lay down and communicate to you with some degree of confidence. I have often given you hints of this kind before, but then it has been by snatches; I will now be more regular and methodical. I shall say nothing with regard to your bodily carriage and address, but leave them to the care of your dancing-master and to your own attention to the best models; remember, however, that they are of consequence.

Talk often, but never long; in that case, if you do not please, at least you are sure not to tire your hearers. Pay your own reckoning, but do not treat the whole company,—this being one of the very few cases in which people do not care to be treated, every one being fully convinced that he has wherewithal to pay.

Tell stories very seldom, and absolutely never but where they are very apt and very short. Omit every circumstance that is not material, and beware of digressions. To have frequent recourse to narrative betrays great want of imagination.

Never hold anybody by the button or the hand in order to be heard out; for if people are not willing to hear you, you had much better hold your tongue than them.

Most long talkers single out some one unfortunate man in company (commonly him whom they observe to be the most silent, or their next neighbor) to whisper, or at least in a half voice to convey a continuity of words to. This is excessively ill bred, and in some degree a fraud, — conversation-stock being a joint and common property. But on the other hand, if one of these unmerciful talkers lays hold of you, hear him with patience, and at least seeming attention, if he is worth obliging, — for nothing will oblige him more than a patient hearing, as nothing would hurt him more than either to leave him in the midst of his discourse, or to discover your impatience under your affliction.

Take, rather than give, the tone of the company you are in. If you have parts, you will show them more or less upon every subject; and if you have not, you had better talk sillily upon a subject of other people's than of your own choosing.

Avoid as much as you can, in mixed companies, argumentative, polemical conversations, — which though they should not, yet certainly do, indispose for a time the contending parties toward each other; and if the controversy grows warm and noisy, endeavor to put an end to it by some genteel levity or joke. I quieted such a conversation-hubbub once by representing to them that though I was persuaded none there present would repeat out of company what passed in it, yet I could not answer for the discretion of the passengers in the street, who must necessarily hear all that was said.

Above all things, and upon all occasions, avoid speaking of yourself, if it be possible. Such is the natural pride and vanity of our hearts that it perpetually breaks out, even in people of the best parts, in all the various modes and figures of the egotism.

Some abruptly speak advantageously of themselves, without either pretence or provocation. They are impudent. Others proceed more artfully as they imagine, and forge accusations against themselves, complain of calumnies which they never heard, in order to justify themselves by exhibiting a catalogue of their many virtues. 'They acknowledge it may indeed seem odd that they should talk in that manner of themselves; it is what they do not like, and what they never would have done, — no, no tortures should ever have forced it from them, if they had not been thus unjustly and monstrously accused! But in these cases justice is surely due to one's self as well as to others, and when our character is attacked, we may say in our own justification what otherwise we never would have said.' This thin veil of modesty drawn before vanity is much too transparent to conceal it even from very moderate discernment.

Others go more modestly and more slyly still (as they think) to work, but in my mind, still more ridiculously. They confess themselves (not without some degree of shame and confusion) into all the cardinal virtues by first degrading them into weaknesses, and then owning their misfortune in being made up of those weaknesses. 'They cannot see people suffer without sympathizing with and endeavoring to help them. They cannot see people want without relieving them, though truly their own circumstances cannot very well afford it. They cannot help speaking truth, though they know all the imprudence of it. In short, they know that with all these weaknesses, they are not fit to live in the world, much less to thrive in it; but they are now too old to change, and must rub on as well as they can.' This sounds too ridiculous and *outré*, almost, for the stage; and yet, take my word for it, you will frequently meet with it upon the common stage of the world. And here I will observe, by the by, that you will often meet with characters in Nature so extravagant, that a discreet poet would not venture to set them upon the stage in their true and high coloring.

This principle of vanity and pride is so strong in human nature that it descends even to the lowest objects; and one often sees people angling for praise, where, admitting all they say to be true (which, by the way, it seldom is), no just praise is to be caught. One man affirms that he has rode post an hundred miles in six hours: probably it is a lie; but supposing it to be true, what then? Why he is a very good post-boy, that is all. Another asserts, and probably not without oaths, that he has drunk six or eight bottles of wine at a sitting; out of charity, I will believe him a liar, for if I do not I must think him a beast.

Such, and a thousand more, are the follies and extravagances which vanity draws people into, and which always defeat their own purpose; and as Waller says, upon another subject, —

> "Make the wretch the most despised
> Where most he wishes to be prized."

The only sure way of avoiding these evils is never to speak of yourself at all. But when, historically, you are obliged to mention yourself, take care not to drop one single word that can directly or indirectly be construed as fishing for applause. Be your character what it will, it will be known; and nobody will take it upon your own word. Never imagine that anything you can say yourself will varnish your defects or add lustre to your perfections; but on the contrary it may, and nine times in ten will, make the former more glaring and the latter obscure. If you are silent upon your own subject, neither envy, indignation, nor ridicule will obstruct or allay the applause which you may really deserve; but if you publish your own panegyric upon any occasion, or in any shape whatsoever, and however artfully dressed or disguised, they will all conspire against you, and you will be disappointed of the very end you aim at.

Take care never to seem dark and mysterious, — which is not only a very unamiable character but a very suspicious one too. If you seem mysterious with others, they will be really so with you, and you will know nothing. The height of abilities is to have *volto sciolto* and *pensieri stretti;* that is, a frank, open, and ingenuous exterior with a prudent interior; to be upon your own guard, and yet by a seeming natural openness to put people off theirs. Depend upon it, nine in ten of every company you are in will avail themselves of every indiscreet and unguarded expression of yours, if they can turn it to their own advantage. A prudent reserve is, therefore, as necessary as a seeming openness is prudent. Always look people in the face when you speak to them; the not doing it is thought to imply conscious guilt. Besides that, you lose the advantage of observing by their countenances what impression your discourse makes upon them. In order to know people's real sentiments, I trust much more to my eyes than to my ears; for they can say whatever they have a mind I should hear, but they can seldom help looking what they have no intention that I should know.

Neither retail nor receive scandal willingly; defamation of others may for the present gratify the malignity of the pride of our hearts, cool reflection will draw very disadvantageous conclusions from such a disposition; and in the case of scandal, as in that of robbery, the receiver is always thought as bad as the thief.

Mimicry, which is the common and favorite amusement of little, low minds, is in the utmost contempt with great ones. It is the lowest and most illiberal of all buffoonery. Pray, neither practise it yourself nor applaud it in others. Besides that, the person mimicked is insulted, and as I have often observed to you before, an insult is never forgiven.

I need not, I believe, advise you to adapt your conversation to the people you are conversing with, — for I suppose you would not, without this caution, have talked upon the same subject, and in the same manner, to a minister of state, a bishop, a philosopher, a captain, and a woman. A man of the world must, like the chameleon, be able to take every different hue, which is by no means a criminal or abject, but a necessary complaisance; for it relates only to manners and not to morals.

One word only as to swearing, and that, I hope and believe, is more than is necessary. You may sometimes hear some people in good company interlard their discourse with oaths, by way of embellishment, as they think; but you must observe too, that those who do so are never those who contribute in any degree to give that company the denomination of good company. They are always subalterns, or people of low education; for that practice, besides that it has no one temptation to plead, is as silly and as illiberal as it is wicked.

Loud laughter is the mirth of the mob, who are only pleased with silly things; for true wit or good sense never excited a laugh since the creation of the world. A man of parts and fashion is therefore only seen to smile, but never heard to laugh.

But to conclude this long letter: all the above-mentioned rules, however carefully you may observe them, will lose half their effect if unaccompanied by the Graces. Whatever you say, if you say it with a supercilious, cynical face, or an embarrassed countenance, or a silly, disconcerted grin, will be ill received. If, into the bargain, *you mutter it, or utter it indistinctly and ungracefully*, it will be still worse received. If your air and address are vulgar, awkward, and *gauche*, you may be esteemed indeed, if you have great intrinsic merit, but you will never please; and without pleasing, you will rise but heavily. Venus among the ancients was synonymous with the Graces, who were always supposed to accompany her; and Horace tells us that even youth, and Mercury, the God of arts and eloquence, would not do without her, —

" Parum comis sine te Juventas Mercuriusque "

They are not inexorable ladies, and may be had, if properly and diligently pursued. Adieu.

XXXI.

FURTHER RULES FOR CONDUCT IN GOOD COMPANY.

BATH, *October* 29, O. S. 1748.

DEAR BOY, — My anxiety for your success increases in proportion as the time approaches of your taking your part upon the great stage of the world. . . . I have long since done mentioning your great religious and moral duties, because I could not make your understanding so bad a compliment as to suppose that you wanted or could receive any new instructions upon these two important points. Mr. Harte, I am sure, has not neglected them; besides, they are so obvious to common sense and reason that commentators may (as they often do) perplex, but cannot make them clearer. My province, therefore, is to supply by my experience your hitherto inevitable inexperience in the ways of the world. People at your age are in a state of natural ebriety, and want rails and *gardefous* wherever they go, to hinder them from breaking their necks. This drunkenness of youth is not only tolerated, but even pleases, if kept within certain bounds of discretion and decency. These bounds are the point which it is difficult for the drunken man himself to find out, and there it is that the experience of a friend may not only serve but save him.

Carry with you, and welcome, into company all the gayety and spirits, but as little of the giddiness, of youth as you can. The former will charm; but the latter will often, though innocently, implacably offend. Inform yourself of the characters and situations of the company before you give way to what your imagination may prompt you to say. There are in all companies more wrong heads than right ones, and many more who deserve than who like censure. Should you therefore expatiate in the praise of some virtue which some in company notoriously want, or declaim against any vice which others are notoriously infected with, your reflections, however general and unapplied, will by being applicable be thought personal, and levelled at those people. This consideration points out to you sufficiently not to be suspicious and captious yourself, nor to suppose that things, because they may be, are therefore meant at you. The manners of well-bred people secure one from those indirect and mean attacks; but if by chance a flippant woman, or a pert coxcomb, lets off anything of that kind, it is much better not to seem to understand than to reply to it.

Cautiously avoid talking of either your own or other people's domestic affairs. Yours are nothing to them but tedious; theirs are nothing to you. The subject is a tender one, and it is odds but that you touch somebody or other's sore place; for in this case there is no trusting to specious appearances, which may be, and often are, so contrary to the real situations of things between men and their wives, parents and their children, seeming friends, etc., that with the best intentions in the world one often blunders disagreeably.

Remember that the wit, humor, and jokes of most mixed companies are local. They thrive in that particular soil, but will not often bear transplanting. Every company is differently circumstanced, has its particular cant and jargon, which may give occasion to wit and mirth within that circle, but would seem flat and insipid in any other, and therefore will not bear repeating. Nothing makes a man look sillier than a pleasantry not relished or not understood; and if he meets with a profound silence when he expected a general applause, or, what is worse, if he is desired to explain the *bon mot*, his awkward and embarrassed situation is easier imagined than described. *A propos* of repeating, take great care never to repeat (I do not mean here the pleasantries) in one company what you hear in another. Things seemingly indifferent may by circulation have much graver consequences than you would imagine. Besides there is a general tacit trust in conversation by which a man is obliged not to report anything out of it, though he is not immediately enjoined secrecy. A retailer of this kind is sure to draw himself into a thousand scrapes and discussions, and to be shyly and uncomfortably received wherever he goes.

You will find in most good company some people who only keep their place there by a contemptible title enough; these are what we call "very good-natured fellows," and the French, *bons diables*. The truth is, they are people without any parts or fancy, and who, having no will of their own, readily assent to, concur in, and applaud whatever is said or done in the company; and adopt with the same alacrity the most virtuous or the most criminal, the wisest or the silliest, scheme that happens to be entertained by the majority of the company. This foolish and often criminal complaisance flows from a foolish cause,— the want of any other merit. I hope that you will hold your place in company by a nobler tenure, and that you will hold it (you can bear a quibble, I believe, yet *in capite*. Have a will and an opinion of your own, and adhere to them steadily; but then do it with good humor, good breeding, and (if you have it) with urbanity; for you have not yet beard enough either to preach or censure.

All other kinds of complaisance are not only blameless but necessary in good company. Not to seem to perceive the little weaknesses and the idle but innocent affectations of the company, but even to flatter them in a certain manner is not only very allowable, but in truth a sort of polite duty. They will be pleased with you if you do, and will certainly not be reformed by you if you do not. For instance; you will find in every *groupe* of company two principal figures, — namely, the fine lady and the fine gentleman, who absolutely give the law of wit, language, fashion, and taste to the rest of that society. There is always a strict and often for the time being a tender alliance between these two figures. The lady looks upon her empire as founded upon the divine right of beauty (and full as good a divine right it is as any king, emperor, or pope can pretend to); she requires, and commonly meets with, unlimited passive obedience. And why should she not meet with it? Her demands go no higher than to have her unquestioned pre-eminence in beauty, wit, and fashion firmly established. Few sovereigns (by the way) are so reasonable. The fine gentleman's claims of right are, *mutatis mutandis*, the same; and though indeed he is not always a wit *de jure*, yet as he is the wit *de facto* of that company, he is entitled to a share of your allegiance; and everybody expects at least as much as they are entitled to, if not something more.

Prudence bids you make your court to these joint sovereigns, and no duty that I know of forbids it. Rebellion here is exceedingly dangerous, and inevitably punished by banishment and immediate forfeiture of all your wit, manners, taste, and fashion; as, on the other hand, a cheerful submission, not without some flattery, is sure to procure you a strong recommendation and most effectual pass throughout all their and probably the neighboring dominions. With a moderate share of sagacity, you will, before you have been half an hour in their company, easily discover those two principal figures, both by the deference which you will observe the whole company pay them, and by that easy, careless, and serene air which their consciousness of power gives them. As in this case, so in all others, aim always at the highest; get always into the highest company, and address yourself particularly to the highest in it. The search after the unattainable philosopher's stone has occasioned a thousand useful discoveries which otherwise would never have been made.

What the French justly call *les manières nobles* are only to be acquired in the very best companies. They are the distinguishing characteristics of men of fashion; people of low education never wear them so close but that some part or other of the original vulgarism appears. *Les manières nobles* equally forbid insolent contempt or low envy and jealousy. Low people in good circumstances, fine clothes, and equipages will insolently show contempt for all those who cannot afford as fine clothes, as good an equipage, and who have not (as their term is) as much money in their pockets; on the other hand, they are gnawed with envy, and cannot help discovering it, of those who surpass them in any of these articles, which are far from being sure criterions of merit. They are likewise jealous of being slighted, and consequently suspicious and captious; they are eager and hot about trifles because trifles were at first their affairs of consequence. *Les manières nobles* imply exactly the reverse of all this. Study them early; you cannot make them too habitual and familiar to you.

XXXII.

IMPORTANCE OF THE GRACES ILLUSTRATED IN A DESIGN OF CARLO MARATTI.—THE DUKE OF MARLBOROUGH.

LONDON, *Nov.* 18, O. S. 1748.

DEAR BOY,— Whatever I see, or whatever I hear, my first consideration is whether it can in any way be useful to you. As a proof of this, I went accidentally the other day into a print-shop, where, among many others, I found one print from a famous design of Carlo Maratti,[1] who died about thirty years ago and was the last eminent painter in Europe. The subject is *il Studio del Disegno*, or the School of Drawing. An old man, supposed to be the master, points to his scholars, who are

[1] The date of his death is Dec. 15, 1713.

variously employed in perspective, geometry, and the observation of the statues of antiquity. With regard to perspective, of which there are some little specimens, he has wrote *tanto che basti*, that is, as much as is sufficient; with regard to geometry, *tanto che basti* again; with regard to the contemplation of the ancient statues there is written, *non mai a bastanza*, — there never can be enough. But in the clouds at the top of the piece are represented the three Graces, with this just sentence written over them: *senza di noi ogni fatica è vana*, — that is, without us all labor is vain. This everybody allows to be true in painting; but all people do not seem to consider, as I hope you will, that this truth is full as applicable to every other art or science, — indeed to everything that is to be said or done. I will send you the print itself by Mr. Eliot when he returns; and I will advise you to make the same use of it that the Roman Catholics say they do of the pictures and images of their Saints, — which is only to remind them of those, for the adoration they disclaim. Nay, I will go further; as the transition from popery to paganism is short and easy, I will classically and poetically advise you to invoke and sacrifice to them every day and all the day. It must be owned that the Graces do not seem to be natives of Great Britain, and I doubt the best of us here have more of the rough than the polished diamond. Since barbarism drove them out of Greece and Rome, they seem to have taken refuge in France, where their temples are numerous and their worship the established one.

Examine yourself seriously why such and such people please and engage you more than such and such others of equal merit, and you will always find that it is because the former have the Graces and the latter not. I have known many a woman with an exact shape and a symmetrical assemblage of beautiful features please nobody; while others with very moderate shapes and features have charmed everybody. Why? Because Venus will not charm so much without her attendant Graces as they will without her. Among men, how often have I seen the most solid merit and knowledge neglected, unwelcome, or even rejected for want of them; while flimsy parts, little knowledge, and less merit introduced by the Graces have been received, cherished, and admired! Even virtue, which is moral beauty, wants some of its charms if unaccompanied by them.

If you ask me how you shall acquire what neither you nor I can define or ascertain, I can only answer — *by observation*. Form yourself with regard to others upon what you feel pleases you in them. I can tell you the importance, the advantage, of having the Graces; but I cannot give them you. I heartily wish I could, and I certainly would; for I do not know a better present that I could make you. To show you that a very wise, philosophical, and retired man thinks upon that subject as I do, who have always lived in the world, I send you by Mr. Eliot the famous Mr. Locke's book upon education, in which you will find the stress that he lays upon the Graces, which he calls (and very truly) good breeding. I have marked all the parts of that book that are worth your attention, for as he begins with the child almost from its birth the parts relative to its infancy would be useless to you. Germany is still less than England the seat of the Graces; however, you had as good not say so while you are there. But the place which you are going to in a great degree is; for I have known as many well-bred, pretty men come from Turin as from any part of Europe. The late King Victor Amedée took great pains to form such of his subjects as were of any consideration both to business and manners. The present king, I am told, follows his example: this however is certain, that in all courts and congresses where there are various foreign ministers, those of the King of Sardinia are generally the ablest, the politest, and *les plus déliés*. You will therefore at Turin have very good models to form yourself upon; and remember that with regard to the best models, as well as to the antique Greek statues in the print, *non mai a bastanza*. Observe every word, look, and motion of those who are allowed to be the most accomplished persons there. Observe their natural and careless but genteel air, their unembarrassed good breeding, their unassuming but yet unprostituted dignity. Mind their decent mirth, their discreet frankness, and that *entregent* which, as much above the frivolous as below the important and the secret, is the proper medium for conversation in mixed companies. I will observe, by the by, that the talent of that light *entregent* is often of great use to a foreign minister,—not only as it helps him to domesticate himself in many families, but also as it enables him to put by and parry some subjects of conversation, which might possibly lay him under difficulties both what to say and how to look.

Of all the men that ever I knew in my life (and I knew him extremely well) the late Duke of Marlborough possessed the Graces in the highest degree, not to say engrossed them; and indeed he got the most by them; for I will venture (contrary to the custom of profound historians, who always assign deep causes for great events) to ascribe the better half of the Duke of Marlborough's greatness and riches to those graces. He was eminently illiterate, wrote bad English and spelled it still worse; he had no share of what is commonly called *parts*, that is, he had no brightness, nothing shining in his genius. He had most undoubtedly an excellent good plain understanding with sound judgment. But these alone would probably have raised him but something higher than they found him, which was page to King James the Second's Queen. There the Graces protected and promoted him; for while he was an Ensign of the Guards the Duchess of Cleveland, then favorite mistress to King Charles the Second, struck by those very graces, gave him five thousand pounds, with which he immediately bought an annuity for his life of five hundred pounds a year of my grandfather Halifax, which was the foundation of his subsequent fortune. His figure was beautiful, but his manner was irresistible by either man or woman. It was by this engaging, graceful manner that he was enabled during all his war to connect the various and jarring powers of the Grand Alliance, and to carry them on to the main object of the war, notwithstanding their private and separate views, jealousies, and wrongheadednesses. Whatever Court he went to (and he was often obliged to go himself to some resty and refractory ones), he as constantly prevailed, and brought them into his measures. The Pensionary Heinsius, a venerable old minister grown gray in business and who had governed the republic of the United Provinces for more than forty years, was absolutely governed by the Duke of Marlborough, as that republic feels to this day. He was always cool, and nobody ever observed the least variation in his countenance; he could refuse more gracefully than other people could grant; and those who went away from him the most dissatisfied as to the substance of their business were yet personally charmed with him and in some degree comforted by his manner. With all his gentleness and gracefulness no man living was more conscious of his situation nor maintained his dignity better.

· · · · · · · · ·

XXXIII.

THE IMPORTANCE OF DRESS.

LONDON, *Dec.* 30, O. S. 1748.

DEAR BOY, — I direct this letter to Berlin, where I suppose it will either find you or at least wait but a very little time for you. I cannot help being anxious for your success at this your first appearance upon the great stage of the world; for though the spectators are always candid enough to give great allowances and to show great indulgence to a new actor, yet from the first impressions which he makes upon them they are apt to decide, in their own minds at least whether he will ever be a good one or not. If he seems to understand what he says, by speaking it properly; if he is attentive to his part, instead of staring negligently about; and if, upon the whole, he seems ambitious to please, they willingly pass over little awkwardnesses and inaccuracies, which they ascribe to a commendable modesty in a young and inexperienced actor. They pronounce that he will be a good one in time; and by the encouragement which they give him, make him so the sooner. This I hope will be your case. You have sense enough to understand your part; a constant attention and ambition to excel in it, with a careful observation of the best actors, will inevitably qualify you, if not for the first, at least for considerable parts.

Your dress (as insignificant a thing as dress is in itself) is now become an object worthy of some attention; for I confess I cannot help forming some opinion of a man's sense and character from his dress, and I believe most people do as well as myself. Any affectation whatsoever in dress implies, in my mind, a flaw in the understanding. Most of our young fellows here display some character or other by their dress; some affect the tremendous, and wear a great and fiercely-cocked hat, an enormous sword, a short waistcoat, and a black cravat; these I should be almost tempted to swear the peace against, in my own defence, if I were not convinced that they are but meek asses in lions' skins. Others go in brown frocks, leather breeches, great oaken cudgels in their hands, their hats uncocked, and their hair unpowdered; and imitate grooms, stage-coachmen, and country bumpkins so well in their outsides, that I do not make the least doubt of their resembling them equally in their insides. A man of sense carefully avoids any particular character in his dress; he is accurately clean for his own sake, but all the rest is for other people's. He dresses as well, and in the same manner, as the people of sense and fashion of the place where he is. If he dresses better as he thinks, that is, more than they, he is a fop; if he dresses worse, he is unpardonably negligent: but of the two, I would rather have a young fellow too much than too little dressed; the excess on that side will wear off with a little age and reflection; but if he is negligent at twenty, he will be a sloven at forty. Dress yourself fine where others are fine, and plain where others are plain; but take care always that your clothes are well made and fit you, for otherwise they will give you a very awkward air. When you are once well dressed for the day think no more of it afterwards; and without any stiffness for fear of discomposing that dress, let all your motions be as easy and natural as if you had no clothes on at all. So much for dress, which I maintain to be a thing of consequence in the polite world.

· · · · · · · · · ·

XXXIV.

ON PREJUDICES.—LIBERTY OF THE PRESS

LONDON, *Feb.* 7, O. S. 1749.

DEAR BOY,—You are now come to an age capable of reflection, and I hope you will do, what however few people at your age do, exert it for your own sake in the search of truth and sound knowledge. I will confess (for I am not unwilling to discover my secrets to you) that it is not many years since I have presumed to reflect for myself. Till sixteen or seventeen I had no reflection, and for many years after that, I made no use of what I had. I adopted the notions of the books I read, or the company I kept, without examining whether they were just or not; and I rather chose to run the risk of easy error than to take the time and trouble of investigating truth. Thus, partly from laziness, partly from dissipation, and partly from the *mauvaise honte* of rejecting fashionable notions, I was (as I have since found) hurried away by prejudices instead of being guided by reason, and quietly cherished error instead of seeking for truth. But since I have taken the trouble of reasoning for myself and have had the courage to own that I do so, you cannot imagine how much my notions of things are altered, and in how different a light I now see them from that in which I formerly viewed them through the deceitful medium of prejudice or authority. Nay, I may possibly still retain many errors, which from long habit have perhaps grown into real opinions; for it is very difficult to distinguish habits, early acquired and long entertained, from the result of our reason and reflection.

My first prejudice (for I do not mention the prejudices of boys and women, such as hobgoblins, ghosts, dreams, spilling salt, etc.) was my classical enthusiasm, which I received from the books I read and the masters who explained them to me. I was convinced there had been no common-sense nor common honesty in the world for these last fifteen hundred years, but that they were totally extinguished with the ancient Greek and Roman governments. Homer and Virgil could have no faults, because they were ancient; Milton and Tasso could have no merit, because they were modern. And I could almost have said with regard to the ancients what Cicero very absurdly and unbecomingly for a philosopher says with regard to Plato, *Cum quo errare malim quam cum aliis recte sentire.* Whereas now, without any extraordinary effort of genius, I have discovered that nature was the same three thousand years ago as it is at present; that men were but men then as well as now; that modes and customs vary often, but that human nature is always the same. And I can no more suppose that men were better, braver, or wiser fifteen hundred or three thousand years ago than I can suppose that the animals or vegetables were better then than they are now. I dare assert too in defiance of the favorers of the ancients that Homer's hero, Achilles, was both a brute and a scoundrel, and consequently an improper character for the hero of an epic poem : he had so little regard for his country that he would not act in defence of it because he had quarrelled with Agamemnon about a strumpet; and then afterwards, animated by private resentment only, he went about killing people basely, I will call it, because he knew himself invulnerable; and yet invulnerable as he was he wore the strongest armor in the world, — which I humbly apprehend to be a blunder, for a horse-shoe clapped to his vulnerable heel would have been sufficient. On the other hand, with submission to the favorers of the moderns, I assert with Mr. Dryden that the Devil is in truth the hero of Milton's poem, — his plan, which he lays, pursues, and at last executes, being the subject of the poem. From all which considerations I impartially conclude that the ancients had their excellences and their defects, their virtues and their vices, just like the moderns; pedantry and affectation of learning decide clearly in favor of the former; vanity and ignorance as peremptorily in favor of the latter. Religious prejudices kept pace with my classical ones, and there was a time when I thought it impossible for the honestest man in the world to be saved out of the pale of the Church of England,[1] — not considering that matters of opinion do not depend upon the will, and that it is as natural and as allowable that another man should differ in

---

[1] In 1716 Chesterfield actively opposed the repeal of an outrageous disabling Act passed by the Tories in Queen Anne's reign against dissenters.

opinion from me as that I should differ from him; and that if we are both sincere, we are both blameless, and should consequently have mutual indulgence for each other.

The next prejudices that I adopted were those of the *beau monde*, in which, as I was determined to shine, I took what are commonly called the genteel vices to be necessary. I had heard them reckoned so, and without further inquiry I believed it, or at least should have been ashamed to have denied it for fear of exposing myself to the ridicule of those whom I considered as the models of fine gentlemen. But I am now neither ashamed nor afraid to assert that those genteel vices, as they are falsely called, are only so many blemishes in the character of even a man of the world and what is called a fine gentleman, and degrade him in the opinions of those very people to whom he hopes to recommend himself by them. Nay, this prejudice often extends so far that I have known people pretend to vices they had not, instead of carefully concealing those they had.

Use and assert your own reason; reflect, examine, and analyze everything, in order to form a sound and mature judgment; let no οὗτος ἔφα impose upon your understanding, mislead your actions, or dictate your conversation. Be early what if you are not, you will when too late wish you had been. Consult your reason betimes; I do not say that it will always prove an unerring guide, for human reason is not infallible, but it will prove the least erring guide that you can follow. Books and conversation may assist it, but adopt neither blindly and implicitly;

try both by that best rule which God has given to direct us, — reason. Of all the troubles, do not decline, as many people do, that of thinking. The herd of mankind can hardly be said to think; their notions are almost all adoptive; and in general I believe it is better that it should be so, as such common prejudices contribute more to order and quiet than their own separate reasonings would do, uncultivated and unimproved as they are. We have many of those useful prejudices in this country which I should be very sorry to see removed. The good Protestant conviction that the Pope is both Antichrist and the W — of Babylon, is a more effectual preservative in this country against popery than all the solid and unanswerable arguments of Chillingworth.

The idle story of the Pretender's having been introduced in a warming-pan into the Queen's bed, though as destitute of all probability as of all foundation, has been much more prejudicial to the cause of Jacobitism than all that Mr. Locke and others have written to show the unreasonableness and absurdity of the doctrines of indefeasible hereditary right and unlimited passive obedience. And that silly, sanguine notion which is firmly entertained here, that one Englishman can beat three Frenchmen, encourages, and has sometimes enabled one Englishman in reality to beat two.

A Frenchman ventures his life with alacrity *pour l'honneur du Roi;* were you to change the object which he has been taught to have in view, and tell him that it was *pour le bien de la patrie*, he would very probably run away. Such gross local prejudices prevail with the herd of mankind, and do not impose upon cultivated, informed, and reflecting minds; but then there are notions equally false, though not so glaringly absurd, which are entertained by people of superior and improved understandings merely for want of the necessary pains to investigate, the proper attention to examine, and the penetration requisite to determine the truth. Those are the prejudices which I would have you guard against by a manly exertion and attention of your reasoning faculty. To mention one instance of a thousand that I could give you,—it is a general prejudice, and has been propagated for these sixteen hundred years, that arts and sciences cannot flourish under an absolute government, and that genius must necessarily be cramped where freedom is restrained. This sounds plausible, but is false in fact. Mechanic arts, as agriculture, etc., will indeed be discouraged, where the profits and property are from the nature of the government insecure; but why the despotism of a government should cramp the genius of a mathematician, an astronomer, a poet, or an orator, I confess I never could discover. It may indeed deprive the poet or the orator of the liberty of treating of certain subjects in the manner they would wish; but it leaves them subjects enough to exert genius upon if they have it.

Can an author with reason complain that he is cramped and shackled if he is not at liberty to publish blasphemy, bawdry, or sedition?—all which are equally prohibited in the freest governments, if they are wise and well-regulated ones. This is the present general complaint of the French authors, but indeed chiefly of the bad ones. No wonder, say they, that England produces so many great geniuses; people there may think as they please, and publish what they think. Very true; but who hinders them from thinking as they please? If indeed they think in a manner destructive of all religion, morality, or good manners, or to the disturbance of the State, an absolute government will certainly more effectually prohibit them from or punish them for publishing such thoughts than a free one could do. But how does that cramp the genius of an epic, dramatic, or lyric poet? Or how does it corrupt the eloquence of an orator, in the pulpit or at the bar?

. . . .

XXXV.

DIGNITY OF MANNERS RECOMMENDED: IN WHAT IT CONSISTS.

LONDON, *Aug.* 10, O. S. 1749.

. . . .

There is a certain dignity of manners absolutely necessary to make even the most valuable character either respected or respectable.

Horse-play, romping, frequent and loud fits of laughter, jokes, waggery, and indiscriminate familiarity will sink both merit and knowledge into a degree of contempt. They compose at most a merry fellow, and a merry fellow was never yet a respectable man. Indiscriminate familiarity either offends your superiors, or else dubs you their dependant and led captain. It gives your inferiors just but troublesome and improper claims of equality. A joker is near akin to a buffoon, and neither of them is the least related to wit. Whoever is either admitted or sought for in company upon any other account than that of his merit and manners, is never respected there but only made use of. We will have such-a-one, for he sings prettily; we will invite such-a-one to a ball, for he dances well; we will have such-a-one at supper, for he is always joking and laughing; we will ask another because he plays deep at all games, or because he can drink a great deal. These are all vilifying distinctions, mortifying preferences, and exclude all ideas of esteem and regard. Whoever *is had* (as it is called) in company for the sake of any one thing singly, is singly that thing, and will never be considered in any other light; consequently never respected, let his merits be what they will.

This dignity of manners which I recommend so much to you is not only as different from pride as true courage is from blustering, or true wit from joking, but is absolutely inconsistent with it; for nothing vilifies and degrades more than pride. The pretensions of the proud man are oftener treated with sneer and contempt than with indignation; as we offer ridiculously too little to a tradesman who asks ridiculously too much for his goods, but we do not haggle with one who only asks a just and reasonable price.

Abject flattery and indiscriminate assentation degrade as much as indiscriminate contradiction and noisy debate disgust. But a modest assertion of one's own opinion and a complaisant acquiescence in other people's preserve dignity.

Vulgar, low expressions, awkward motions and address, vilify; as they imply either a very low turn of mind or low education and low company.

Frivolous curiosity about trifles and laborious attention to little objects, which neither require nor deserve a moment's thought, lower a man; who from thence is thought (and not unjustly) incapable of greater matters. Cardinal de Retz very sagaciously marked out Cardinal Chigi for a little mind from the moment that he told him he had wrote three years with the same pen, and that it was an excellent good one still.

. . . .

XXXVI.

COURT MANNERS AND METHODS.

Aug. 21, O. S. 1749.

. . . .

You will soon be at Courts, where though you will not be concerned, yet reflection and observation upon what you see and hear there may be of use to you when hereafter you may come to be concerned in courts yourself. Nothing in courts is exactly as it appears to be, — often very different, sometimes directly contrary. Interest, which is the real spring of everything there, equally creates and dissolves friendship, produces and reconciles enmities; or rather, allows of neither real friendships nor enmities; for as Dryden very justly observes, " Politicians neither love nor hate." This is so true that you may think you connect yourself with two friends to-day and be obliged to-morrow to make your option between them as enemies. Observe therefore such a degree of reserve with your friends as not to put yourself in their power if they should become your enemies, and such a degree of moderation with your enemies as not to make it impossible for them to become your friends.

Courts are unquestionably the seats of politeness and good breeding; were they not so, they would be the seats of slaughter and desolation. Those who now smile upon and embrace, would affront and stab each other, if manners did not interpose; but ambition and avarice, the two prevailing passions at courts, found dissimulation more effectual than violence; and dissimulation introduced that habit of politeness which distinguishes the courtier from the country gentleman. In the former case the strongest body would prevail; in the latter, the strongest mind.

A man of parts and efficiency need not flatter everybody at court, but he must take great care to offend nobody personally, it being in the power of very many to hurt him who cannot serve him. Homer supposes a chain let down from Jupiter to the earth to connect him with mortals. There is at all courts a chain which connects the prince or the minister with the page of the backstairs or the chambermaid. The king's wife, or mistress, has an influence over him; a lover has an influence over her; the chambermaid or the valet de chambre has an influence over both; and so *ad infinitum*. You must therefore not break a link of that chain by which you hope to climb up to the prince.

. . . .

XXXVII.

ON AWKWARDNESS AND ABSENCE OF MIND.—DRESS.

LONDON, *Sept.* 22, O. S. 1749.

DEAR BOY,—If I had faith in philters and love potions I should suspect that you had given Sir Charles Williams some by the manner in which he speaks of you, not only to me but to everybody else. I will not repeat to you what he says of the extent and correctness of your knowledge, as it might either make you vain or persuade you that you had already enough of what nobody can have too much. You will easily imagine how many questions I asked, and how narrowly I sifted him upon your subject; he answered me, and I dare say with truth, just as I could have wished, till, satisfied entirely with his accounts of your character and learning, I inquired into other matters intrinsically indeed of less consequence but still of great consequence to every man, and of more to you than to almost any man,—I mean your address, manners, and air. To these questions the same truth which he had observed before obliged him to give me much less satisfactory answers. And as he thought himself in friendship both to you and me obliged to tell me the disagreeable as well as the agreeable truths, upon the same principle I think myself obliged to repeat them to you.

He told me then that in company you were frequently most *provokingly* inattentive, absent, and *distrait;* that you came into a room and presented yourself very awkwardly; that at table you constantly threw down knives, forks, napkins, bread, etc., and that you neglected your person and dress to a degree unpardonable at any age, and much more so at yours.

These things, howsoever immaterial they may seem to people who do not know the world and the nature of mankind, give me, who know them to be exceedingly material, very great concern. I have long distrusted you and therefore frequently admonished you upon these articles; and I tell you plainly that I shall not be easy till I hear a very different account of them. I know no one thing more offensive to a company than that inattention and *distraction*. It is showing them the utmost contempt, and people never forgive contempt. No man is *distrait* with the man he fears or the woman he loves; which is a proof that every man can get the better of that *distraction* when he thinks it worth his while to do so, and take my word for it it is always worth his while. For my own part I would rather be in company with a dead man than with an absent one; for if the dead man gives me no pleasure, at least he shows me no contempt; whereas the absent man, silently indeed but very plainly, tells me that he does not think me worth his attention. Besides, can an absent man make any observations upon the characters, customs, and manners of the company? No. He may be in the best companies all his lifetime (if they will admit him which if I were they I would not) and never be one jot the wiser. I never will converse with an absent man; one may as well talk to a deaf one. It is in truth a practical blunder to address ourselves to a man who we see plainly neither hears, minds, nor understands us. Moreover, I aver that no man is in any degree fit for either business or conversation who cannot and does not direct and command his attention to the present object, be that what it will. You know by experience that I grudge no expense in your education, but I will positively not keep you a flapper. You may read in Dr. Swift the description of these flappers and the use they were of to your friends the Laputans, whose minds (Gulliver says) are so taken up with intense speculations that they neither can speak nor attend to the discourses of others without being roused by some external taction upon the organs of speech and hearing; for which reason those people who are able to afford it always keep a flapper in their family as one of their domestics, nor ever walk about or make visits without him. This flapper is likewise employed diligently to attend his master in his walks, and upon occasion to give a soft flap upon his eyes, because he is always so wrapped up in cogitation that he is in manifest danger of falling down every precipice and bouncing his head against every post, and in the streets of jostling others or being jostled into the kennel himself. If *Christian* will undertake this province into the bargain, with all my heart; but I will not allow him any increase of wages upon that score. In short, I give you fair warning that when we meet, if you are absent in mind I will soon be absent in body, for it will be impossible for me to stay in the room; and if at table you throw down your knife, plate, bread, etc., and hack the wing of a chicken for half an hour without being able to cut it off, and your sleeve all the time in another dish, I must rise from table to escape the fever you would certainly give me. Good God! how I should be shocked if you came into my room for the first time with two left legs, presenting yourself with all the graces and dignity of a tailor, and your clothes hanging upon you like those in Monmouth Street, upon tenter-hooks! whereas I expect, nay, require to see you present yourself with the easy and genteel air of a man of fashion who has kept good company. I expect you not only well dressed but very well dressed; I expect a gracefulness in all your motions and something particularly engaging in your address. All this I expect, and all this it is in your power, by care and attention, to make me find; but to tell you the plain truth, if I do not find it we shall not converse very much together, for I cannot stand inattention and awkwardness, — it would endanger my health. You have often seen and I have as often made you observe L——'s[1] distinguished inattention and awkwardness. Wrapped up like a Laputan in intense thought, and possibly sometimes in no thought at all (which I believe is very often the case with absent people), he does not know his most intimate acquaintance by sight or answers them as if he were at cross purposes. He leaves his hat in one room, his sword in another, and would leave his shoes in a third, if his buckles though awry did not save them; his legs and arms by his awkward management of them seem to have undergone the *question extraordinaire;* and his head always hanging upon one or other of his shoulders seems to have received the first stroke upon a block. I sincerely value and esteem him for his parts, learning, and virtue, but for the soul of me I cannot love him in company. This will be universally the case in common life of every inattentive awkward man, let his real merit and knowledge be ever so great. When I was of your age I desired to shine as far as I was able in every part of life, and was as attentive to my manners, my dress, and my air in company of evenings as to my books and my tutor in the mornings. A young fellow should be ambitious to shine in everything, and of the two always rather overdo than underdo. These things are by no means trifles; they are of infinite consequence to those who are to be thrown into the great world and who would make a figure or a fortune in it. It is not sufficient to deserve

[1] Lord Lyttleton.

well; one must please well too. Awkward, disagreeable merit will never carry anybody far. Wherever you find a good dancing-master, pray let him put you upon your haunches; not so much for the sake of dancing as for coming into a room and presenting yourself genteelly and gracefully. Women, whom you ought to endeavor to please, cannot forgive vulgar and awkward air and gestures; *il leur faut du brillant.* The generality of men are pretty like them, and are equally taken by the same exterior graces.

I am very glad that you have received the diamond buckles safe; all I desire in return for them is that they may be buckled even upon your feet and that your stockings may not hide them. I should be sorry that you were an egregious fop, but I protest that of the two I would rather have you a fop than a sloven. I think negligence in my own dress, even at my age when certainly I expect no advantages from my dress, would be indecent with regard to others. I have done with fine clothes, but I will have my plain clothes fit me and made like other people's. In the evenings I recommend to you the company of women of fashion, who have a right to attention and will be paid it. Their company will smooth your manners and give you a habit of attention and respect, of which you will find the advantage among men.

. . . . . .

XXXVIII.

VULGARISMS. — AN AWKWARD MAN. — THE MAN OF TASTE.

LONDON, *Sept.* 27, O. S. 1749.

DEAR BOY, — A vulgar ordinary way of thinking, acting, or speaking implies a low education and a habit of low company. Young people contract it at school, or among servants, with whom they are too often used to converse; but after they frequent good company, they must want attention and observation very much if they do not lay it quite aside. And indeed if they do not, good company will be very apt to lay them aside. The various kinds of vulgarisms are infinite; I cannot pretend to point them out to you, but I will give some samples by which you may guess at the rest.

A vulgar man is captious and jealous, eager and impetuous about trifles. He suspects himself to be slighted, thinks everything that is said meant at him. If the company happens to laugh, he is persuaded they laugh at him; he grows angry and testy, says something very impertinent, and draws himself into a scrape by showing what he calls a proper spirit and asserting himself. A man of fashion does not suppose himself to be either the sole or principal object of the thoughts, looks, or words of the company; and never suspects that he is either slighted or laughed at, unless he is conscious that he deserves it. And if (which very seldom happens) the company is absurd or ill bred enough to do either, he does not care twopence, unless the insult be so gross and plain as to require satisfaction of another kind. As he is above trifles, he is never vehement and eager about them; and wherever they are concerned rather acquiesces than wrangles. A vulgar man's conversation always savors strongly of the lowness of his education and company. It turns chiefly upon his domestic affairs, his servants, the excellent order he keeps in his own family, and the little anecdotes of the neighborhood; all which he relates with emphasis as interesting matters. He is a man gossip.

Vulgarism in language is the next and distinguishing characteristic of bad company and a bad education. A man of fashion avoids nothing with more care than that. Proverbial expressions and trite sayings are the flowers of the rhetoric of a vulgar man. Would he say that men differ in their tastes, he both supports and adorns that opinion by the good old saying, as he respectfully calls it, that " what is one man's meat is another man's poison." If anybody attempts being " smart," as he calls it, upon him, he gives them " Tit for Tat," ay, that he does. He has always some favorite word for the time being, which for the sake of using often he commonly abuses: such as *vastly* angry, *vastly* kind, *vastly* handsome, and *vastly* ugly. Even his pronunciation of proper words carries the mark of the beast along with it. He calls the earth *yearth;* he is *obleiged* not *obliged* to you. He goes *to wards* and not *towards* such a place. He sometimes affects hard words by way of ornament, which he always mangles, like a learned woman. A man of fashion never has recourse to proverbs and vulgar aphorisms; uses neither favorite words nor hard words, but takes great care to speak very correctly and grammatically, and to pronounce properly, — that is, according to the usage of the best companies.

An awkward address, ungraceful attitudes and actions, and a certain left-handedness (if I may use that word), loudly proclaim low education and low company; for it is impossible to suppose that a man can have frequented good company without having catched something at least of their air and motions. A new-raised man is distinguished in a regiment by his awkwardness; but he must be impenetrably dull if in a month or two's time he cannot perform at least the common manual exercise and look like a soldier. The very accoutrements of a man of fashion are grievous encumbrances to a vulgar man. He is at a loss what to do with his hat when it is not upon his head; his cane (if unfortunately he wears one) is at perpetual war with every cup of tea or coffee he drinks, — destroys them first, and then accompanies them in their fall. His sword is formidable only to his own legs, which would possibly carry him fast enough out of the way of any sword but his own. His clothes fit him so ill, and constrain him so much, that he seems rather their prisoner than their proprietor. He presents himself in company like a criminal in a court of justice; his very air condemns him, and people of fashion will no more connect themselves with the one than people of character will with the other. This repulse drives and sinks him into low company, a gulf from whence no man, after a certain age, ever emerged.

Les manières nobles et aisées, la tournure d'un homme de condition, le ton de la bonne compagnie, les graces, le je ne sais quoi qui plaît, are as necessary to adorn and introduce your intrinsic merit and knowledge as the polish is to the diamond, which without that polish would never be worn, whatever it might weigh. Do not imagine that these accomplishments are only useful with women; they are much more so with men. In a public assembly what an advantage has a graceful speaker with genteel motions, a handsome figure, and a liberal air, over one who shall speak full as much good sense but destitute of these ornaments! In business how prevalent are the Graces, how detrimental is the want of them! By the help of these I have known some men refuse favors less offensively than others granted them. The utility of them in Courts and negotiations is inconceivable. You gain the hearts and consequently the secrets of nine in ten that you have to do with in spite even of their prudence, — which will nine times in ten be the dupe of their hearts and of their senses. Consider the importance of these things as they deserve and you will not lose one minute in the pursuit of them.

You are travelling now in a country[1] once so famous both for arts and arms that (however degen-

[1] Italy.

erate at present) it still deserves your attention and reflection. View it therefore with care, compare its former with its present state, and examine into the causes of its rise and its decay. Consider it classically and politically, and do not run through it, as too many of your young countrymen do, musically and (to use a ridiculous word) *knick-knackically*. No piping nor fiddling, I beseech you; no days lost in poring upon almost imperceptible *intaglios* and *cameos;* and do not become a virtuoso of small wares. Form a taste of painting, sculpture, and architecture, if you please, by a careful examination of the works of the best ancient and modern artists; those are liberal arts, and a real taste and knowledge of them become a man of fashion very well. But beyond certain bounds the man of taste ends, and the frivolous virtuoso begins.

. . . .

XXXIX.

THREE SORTS OF GOOD BREEDING

LONDON, *Nov.* 3, O. S. 1749.

DEAR BOY, — From the time that you have had life, it has been the principal and favorite object of mine to make you as perfect as the imperfections of human nature will allow; in this view I have grudged no pains nor expense in your education, convinced that education more than nature is the cause of that great difference which you see in the characters of men. While you were a child, I endeavored to form your heart habitually to virtue and honor before your understanding was capable of showing you their beauty and utility. Those principles which you then got, like your grammar rules, only by rote, are now I am persuaded fixed and confirmed by reason. And indeed they are so plain and clear that they require but a very moderate degree of understanding either to comprehend or practise them. Lord Shaftesbury says very prettily that he would be virtuous for his own sake though nobody were to know it, as he would be clean for his own sake though nobody were to see him. I have therefore, since you have had the use of your reason, never written to you upon those subjects; they speak best for themselves; and I should now just as soon think of warning you gravely not to fall into the dirt or the fire as into dishonor or vice. This view of mine I consider as fully attained. My next object was sound and useful learning. My own care first, Mr. Harte's afterwards, and *of late* (I will own it to your praise) your own application have more than answered my expectations in that particular, and I have reason to believe will answer even my wishes. All that remains for me then to wish, to recommend, to inculcate, to order, and to insist upon is good breeding, without which all your other qualifications will be lame, unadorned, and to a certain degree unavailing. And here I fear and have too much reason to believe that you are greatly deficient. The remainder of this letter, therefore, shall be (and it will not be the last by a great many) upon that subject.

A friend of yours and mine has very justly defined

good breeding to be " the result of much good sense, some good-nature, and a little self-denial for the sake of others, and with a view to obtain the same indulgence from them." Taking this for granted (as I think it cannot be disputed), it is astonishing to me that anybody who has good sense and good-nature (and I believe you have both) can essentially fail in good breeding. As to the modes of it indeed they vary according to persons and places and circumstances, and are only to be acquired by observation and experience; but the substance of it is everywhere and eternally the same. Good manners are to particular societies what good morals are to society in general, — their cement and their security. And as laws are enacted to enforce good morals, or at least to prevent the ill effects of bad ones, so there are certain rules of civility universally implied and received to enforce good manners and punish bad ones. And indeed there seems to me to be less difference both between the crimes and between the punishments than at first one would imagine. The immoral man who invades another man's property is justly hanged for it; and the ill bred man who by his ill manners invades and disturbs the quiet and comforts of private life is by common consent as justly banished society. Mutual complaisances, attentions, and sacrifices of little conveniences are as natural an implied compact between civilized people as protection and obedience are between kings and subjects; whoever in either case violates that compact justly forfeits all advantages arising from it. For my own part, I really think that next to the consciousness of doing a good action, that of doing a civil one is the most pleasing; and the epithet which I should covet the most, next to that of Aristides, would be that of well-bred. Thus much for good breeding in general; I will now consider some of the various modes and degrees of it.

Very few, scarcely any, are wanting in the respect which they should show to those whom they acknowledge to be infinitely their superiors, — such as crowned heads, princes, and public persons of distinguished and eminent posts. It is the manner of showing that respect which is different. The man of fashion and of the world expresses it in its fullest extent, but naturally, easily, and without concern; whereas a man who is not used to keep good company, expresses it awkwardly. One sees that he is not used to it, and that it costs him a great deal; but I never saw the worst-bred man living guilty of lolling, whistling, scratching his head, and such-like indecencies in company that he respected. In such companies, therefore, the only point to be attended to is to show that respect which everybody means to show in an easy, unembarrassed, and graceful manner. This is what observation and experience must teach you.

In mixed companies whoever is admitted to make part of them is for the time at least supposed to be upon a footing of equality with the rest; and consequently as there is no one principal object of awe and respect, people are apt to take a greater latitude in their behavior and to be less upon their guard; and so they may, provided it be within certain bounds which are upon no occasion to be transgressed. But upon these occasions, though no one is entitled to distinguished marks of respect, every one claims, and very justly, every mark of civility and good breeding. Ease is allowed, but carelessness and negligence are strictly forbidden. If a man accosts you and talks to you ever so dully or frivolously, it is worse than rudeness, it is brutality to show him by a manifest inattention to what he says that you think him a fool or a blockhead, and not worth hearing. It is much more so with regard to women; who, of whatever rank they are, are entitled in consideration of their sex not only to an attentive but an officious good breeding from men. Their little wants, likings, dislikes, preferences, antipathies, fancies, whims, and even impertinencies must be officiously attended to, flattered, and if possible, guessed at and anticipated by a well-bred man. You must never usurp to yourself those conveniences and *agrémens* which are of common right, such as the best places, the best dishes, etc., but on the contrary always decline them yourself and offer them to others, who in their turns will offer them to you; so that upon the whole you will in your turn enjoy your share of the common right. It would be endless for me to enumerate all the particular instances in which a well-bred man shows his good breeding in good company, and it would be injurious to you to suppose that your own good sense will not point them out to you; and then your own good-nature will recommend, and your self-interest enforce the practice.

There is a third sort of good breeding in which

people are the most apt to fail from a very mistaken notion that they cannot fail at all, — I mean with regard to one's most familiar friends and acquaintances, or those who really are our inferiors; and there undoubtedly a greater degree of ease is not only allowed but proper, and contributes much to the comforts of a private social life. But that ease and freedom have their bounds too, which must by no means be violated. A certain degree of negligence and carelessness becomes injurious and insulting from the real or supposed inferiority of the persons; and that delightful liberty of conversation among a few friends is soon destroyed, as liberty often has been, by being carried to licentiousness. But example explains things best, and I will put a pretty strong case. Suppose you and me alone together; I believe you will allow that I have as good a right to unlimited freedom in your company as either you or I can possibly have in any other, and I am apt to believe too that you would indulge me in that freedom as far as anybody would. But notwithstanding this, do you imagine that I should think there were no bounds to that freedom? I assure you I should not think so; and I take myself to be as much tied down by a certain degree of good manners to you as by other degrees of them to other people. Were I to show you by a manifest inattention to what you said to me that I was thinking of something else the whole time; were I to yawn extremely or snore in your company, I should think that I behaved myself to you like a beast and should not expect that you would care to frequent me. No; the most familiar and intimate habitudes, connections, and friendships require a degree of good breeding both to preserve and cement them. If ever a man and his wife, who pass nights as well as days together, absolutely lay aside all good breeding, their intimacy will soon degenerate into a coarse familiarity infallibly productive of contempt or disgust. The best of us have our bad sides, and it is as imprudent as it is ill bred to exhibit them. I shall certainly not use ceremony with you; it would be misplaced between us; but I shall certainly observe that degree of good breeding with you which is in the first place decent, and which I am sure is absolutely necessary to make us like one another's company long.

I will say no more now upon this important subject of good breeding, which I have already dwelt upon too long, it may be, for one letter, and upon which I shall frequently refresh your memory hereafter; but I will conclude with these axioms:

That the deepest learning without good breeding is unwelcome and tiresome pedantry and of no use nowhere but in a man's own closet, and consequently, of little or no use at all.

That a man who is not perfectly well bred is unfit for good company and unwelcome in it, will consequently dislike it soon, afterwards renounce it; and be reduced to solitude or (what is worse) low and bad company.

That a man who is not well bred is full as unfit for business as for company.

Make then, my dear child, I conjure you, good breeding the great object of your thoughts and actions, at least half the day. Observe carefully the behavior and manners of those who are distinguished by their good breeding; imitate, nay, endeavor to excel, that you may at last reach them; and be convinced that good breeding is to all worldly qualifications what charity is to all Christian virtues. Observe how it adorns merit, and how often it covers the want of it. May you wear it to adorn and not to cover you! Adieu.

XL.

THE SAME SUBJECT CONTINUED.

LONDON, *Nov.* 14, O S. 1749.

DEAR BOY, — There is a natural good breeding which occurs to every man of common-sense and is practised by every man of common good-nature. This good breeding is general, independent of modes, and consists in endeavors to please and oblige our fellow-creatures by all good offices short of moral duties. This will be practised by a good-natured American savage as essentially as by the best-bred European. But then I do not take it to extend to the sacrifice of our own conveniences for the sake of other people's. Utility introduced this sort of good breeding as it introduced commerce, and established a truck[1] of the little *agrémens* and

---

[1] Barter.

pleasures of life. I sacrifice such a conveniency to you, you sacrifice another to me; this commerce circulates, and every individual finds his account in it upon the whole. The third sort of good breeding is local and is variously modified in not only different countries but in different towns of the same country. But it must be founded upon the two former sorts; they are the matter to which, in this case, fashion and custom only give the different shapes and impressions. Whoever has the two first sorts will easily acquire this third sort of good breeding, which depends singly upon attention and observation. It is properly the polish, the lustre, the last finishing stroke of good breeding. It is to be found only in capitals, and even there it varies, — the good breeding of Rome differing in some things from that of Paris; that of Paris in others from that of Madrid; and that of Madrid in many things from that of London. A man of sense, therefore, carefully attends to the local manners of the respective places where he is and takes for his models those persons whom he observes to be at the head of fashion and good breeding. He watches how they address themselves to their superiors, how they accost their equals, and how they treat their inferiors; and lets none of those little niceties escape him which are to good breeding what the last delicate and masterly touches are to a good picture, and of which the vulgar have no notion, but by which good judges distinguish the master. He attends even to their air, dress, and motions, and imitates them liberally and not servilely; he copies but does not mimic. These personal graces are of very great consequence. They anticipate the sentiments before merit can engage the understanding; they captivate the heart, and gave rise I believe to the extravagant notions of charms and philters. Their effects were so surprising that they were reckoned supernatural. The most graceful and best-bred men and the handsomest and genteelest women give the most philters, and as I verily believe without the least assistance of the devil. Pray be not only well dressed but shining in your dress; let it have *du brillant;* I do not mean by a clumsy load of gold and silver, but by the taste and fashion of it. Women like and require it; they think it an attention due to them. But on the other hand if your motions and carriage are not graceful, genteel, and natural, your fine clothes will only display your awkwardness the more. But I am unwilling to suppose you still awkward, for surely by this time you must have catched a good air in good company. When you went from hence you were naturally awkward, but your awkwardness was adventitious and Westmonasterial. Leipsic, I apprehend, is not the seat of the Graces, and I presume you acquired none there. But now if you will be pleased to observe what people of the first fashion do with their legs and arms, heads and bodies, you will reduce yours to certain decent laws of motion. You danced pretty well here and ought to dance very well before you come home; for what one is obliged to do sometimes one ought to be able to do well. Besides, *la belle danse donne du brillant à un jeune homme*, and you should endeavor to shine. A calm serenity, negative merit and graces, do not become your age. You should be *alerte, adroit, vif;* be wanted, talked of, impatiently expected, and unwillingly parted with in company. I should be glad to hear half a dozen women of fashion say, " Où est donc le petit Stanhope? Que ne vient-il? Il faut avouer qu'il est aimable." All this I do not mean singly with regard to women as the principal object, but with regard to men and with a view of your making yourself considerable. For with very small variations the same things that please women please men, and a man whose manners are softened and polished by women of fashion and who is formed by them to an habitual attention and complaisance, will please, engage, and connect men much easier and more than he would otherwise. You must be sensible that you cannot rise in the world without forming connections and engaging different characters to conspire in your point. You must make them your dependants without their knowing it, and dictate to them while you seem to be directed by them. Those necessary connections can never be formed or preserved but by an uninterrupted series of complaisance, attentions, politeness, and some constraint. You must engage their hearts if you would have their support ; you must watch the *mollia tempora,* and captivate them by the *agrémens* and charms of conversation. People will not be called out to your service only when you want them ; and if you expect to receive strength from them, they must receive either pleasure or advantage from you.

. . . .

XLI.

GOOD BREEDING IMPORTANT IN DIPLOMACY. — CIVILITY TOWARD WOMEN. — ILLUSTRATION DRAWN FROM ARCHITECTURE.

[*No date.*]

DEAR BOY, — My last was upon the subject of good breeding, but I think it rather set before you the unfitness and disadvantages of ill breeding than the utility and necessity of good; it was rather negative than positive. This therefore should go further and explain to you the necessity which you of all people living lie under, not only of being positively and actively well bred but of shining and distinguishing yourself by your good breeding. Consider your own situation in every particular and judge whether it is not essentially your interest by your own good breeding to others to secure theirs to you; and that, let me assure you, is the only way of doing it; for people will repay, and with interest too, inattention with inattention, neglect with neglect, and ill manners with worse, — which may engage you in very disagreeable affairs. In the next place your profession requires more than any other the nicest and most distinguished good breeding. You will negotiate with very little success if you do not previously by your manners conciliate and engage the affections of those with whom you are to negotiate. Can you ever get into the confidence and the secrets of the Courts where you may happen to reside, if you have not those pleasing, insinuating manners which alone can procure them? Upon my word I do not say too much when I say that superior good breeding, insinuating manners, and genteel address are half your business. Your knowledge will have but very little influence upon the mind if your manners prejudice the heart against you; but on the other hand, how easily will you dupe the understanding where you have first engaged the heart! and hearts are by no means to be gained by that mere common civility which everybody practises. Bowing again to those who bow to you, answering dryly those who speak to you, and saying nothing offensive to anybody is such negative good breeding that it is only not being a brute. It is an active, cheerful, officious, seducing good breeding that must gain you the good will and first sentiments of men and the affections of the women. You must carefully watch and attend to their passions, their tastes, their little humors and weaknesses, and *aller au devant*. You must do it at the same time with alacrity and *empressement*, and not as if you graciously condescended to humor their weaknesses.

For instance, suppose you invited anybody to dine or sup with you, you ought to recollect if you had observed that they had any favorite dish and take care to provide it for them: and when it came you should say, "You seemed to me at such and such a place to give this dish a preference, and therefore I ordered it. This is the wine that I observed you liked and therefore I procured some." The more trifling these things are the more they prove your attention for the person and are consequently the more engaging. Consult your own breast and recollect how these little attentions when shown you by others flatter that degree of self-love and vanity from which no man living is free. Reflect how they incline and attract you to that person and how you are propitiated afterwards to all which that person says or does. The same causes will have the same effects in your favor. Women in a great degree establish or destroy every man's reputation of good breeding; you must, therefore, in a manner overwhelm them with these attentions, — they are used to them, they expect them, and to do them justice, they commonly requite them. You must be sedulous and rather over-officious than under in procuring them their coaches, their chairs, their conveniences in public places; not see what you should not see, and rather assist where you cannot help seeing. Opportunities of showing these attentions present themselves perpetually; but if they do not, make them. As Ovid advises his lover, when he sits in the Circus near his mistress, to wipe the dust off her neck even if there be none: "Si nullus, tamen excute nullum." Your conversation with women should always be respectful, but at the same time *enjoué*, and always addressed to their vanity. Everything you say or do should convince them of the regard you have (whether you have it or not) for their beauty, their wit, or their merit.

Men have possibly as much vanity as women, though of another kind; and both art and good breeding require that instead of mortifying, you should please and flatter it by words and looks of approbation. Suppose (which is by no means improbable) that at your return to England I should place you near the person of some one of the royal family; in that situation, good breeding, engaging address, adorned with all the graces that dwell at Courts, would very probably make you a favorite and from a favorite a minister; but all the knowledge and learning in the world without them never would. The penetration of princes seldom goes deeper than the surface. It is the exterior that always engages their hearts, and I would never advise you to give yourself much trouble about their understanding. Princes in general (I mean those *Porphyrogenets*[1] who are born and bred in purple) are about the pitch of women, bred up like them, and are to be addressed and gained in the same manner. They always see, they seldom weigh. Your lustre, not your solidity, must take them; your inside will afterwards support and secure what your outside has acquired. With weak people (and they undoubtedly are three parts in four of mankind) good breeding, address, and manners are everything; they can go no deeper; but let me assure you that they are a great deal even

[1] An apartment of the Byzantine palace was lined with porphyry; it was reserved for the use of the pregnant empresses, and the royal birth of their children was expressed by the appellation of "Porphyrogenite," or Born in the Purple. — GIBBON: *Decline and Fall of the Roman Empire*, ch. xlviii.

with people of the best understandings. Where the eyes are not pleased and the heart is not flattered, the mind will be apt to stand out. Be this right or wrong, I confess I am so made myself. Awkwardness and ill breeding shock me to that degree, that where I meet with them I cannot find in my heart to inquire into the intrinsic merit of that person; I hastily decide in myself that he can have none, and am not sure that I should not even be sorry to know that he had any. I often paint you in my imagination in your present *lontananza*, and while I view you in the light of ancient and modern learning, useful and ornamental knowledge, I am charmed with the prospect; but when I view you in another light, and represent you awkward, ungraceful, ill bred, with vulgar air and manners, shambling towards me with inattention and *distractions*, I shall not pretend to describe to you what I feel, but will do as a skilful painter did formerly, — draw a veil before the countenance of the father.[1]

I dare say you know already enough of Architecture to know that the Tuscan is the strongest and most solid of all the Orders; but at the same time, it is the coarsest and clumsiest of them. Its solidity does extremely well for the foundation and base floor of a great edifice; but if the whole building be Tuscan, it will attract no eyes, it will stop no passengers, it will invite no interior examination. People will take it for granted that the finishing and furnishing cannot be worth seeing where the front is so unadorned

[1] Probably an allusion to Timanthes' painting of the sacrifice of Iphigeneia.

and clumsy. But if upon the solid Tuscan foundation, the Doric, the Ionic, and the Corinthian Orders rise gradually with all their beauty, proportions, and ornaments, the fabric seizes the most incurious eye and stops the most careless passenger, who solicits admission as a favor, nay, often purchases it. Just so will it fare with your little fabric, which at present I fear has more of the Tuscan than of the Corinthian Order. You must absolutely change the whole front, or nobody will knock at the door. The several parts which must compose this new front are elegant, easy, natural, superior good breeding; an engaging address; genteel motions; an insinuating softness in your looks, words, and actions; a spruce, lively air, fashionable dress; and all the glitter that a young fellow should have.

I am sure you would do a great deal for my sake; and therefore consider, at your return here, what a disappointment and concern it would be to me, if I could not safely depute you to do the honors of my house and table, and if I should be ashamed to present you to those who frequent both. Should you be awkward, inattentive, and *distrait*, and happen to meet Mr. L [yttleton] at my table, the consequences of that meeting must be fatal; you would run your heads against each other, cut each other's fingers instead of your meat, or die by the precipitate infusion of scalding soup.

This is really so copious a subject that there is no end of being either serious or ludicrous upon it. It is impossible, too, to enumerate or state to you the various cases in good breeding; they are infinite.

There is no situation or relation in the world so remote or so intimate that does not require a degree of it. Your own good sense must point it out to you; your own good-nature must incline, and your interest prompt you to practise it; and observation and experience must give you the manner, the air, and the graces which complete the whole.

. . . .

I have often asserted that the profoundest learning and the politest manners were by no means incompatible, though so seldom found united in the same person; and I have engaged myself to exhibit you as a proof of the truth of this assertion. Should you, instead of that, happen to disprove me, the concern indeed would be mine, but the loss will be yours. Lord Bolingbroke is a strong instance on my side of the question; he joins to the deepest erudition the most elegant politeness and good breeding that ever any courtier and man of the world was adorned with, and Pope very justly called him "all-accomplished St. John," with regard to his knowledge and his manners. He had, it is true, his faults, which proceeded from unbounded ambition and impetuous passions, but they have now subsided by age and experience; and I can wish you nothing better than to be what he is now, without being what he has been formerly. His address pre-engages, his eloquence persuades, and his knowledge informs all who approach him. Upon the whole, I do desire and insist that from after dinner till you go to bed, you make good breeding, address, and manners your serious object and your only care. Without them, you will be nobody; with them, you may be anything.

Adieu, my dear child. My compliments to Mr. Harte.

XLII.

GREAT EVENTS FROM TRIVIAL CAUSES. — HOW TO SHINE AS AN ORATOR.

LONDON, *Dec.* 5, O. S. 1749.

DEAR BOY, — Those who suppose that men in general act rationally because they are called rational creatures know very little of the world, and if they act themselves upon that supposition will nine times in ten find themselves grossly mistaken. That man is *animal bipes, implume, risibile*, I entirely agree; but for the *rationale*, I can only allow it him *in actu primo* (to talk logic) and seldom *in actu secundo*. Thus the speculative, cloistered pedant in his solitary cell forms systems of things as they should be, not as they are; and writes as decisively and absurdly upon war, politics, manners, and characters as that pedant talked who was so kind as to instruct Hannibal in the art of war. Such closet politicians never fail to assign the deepest motives for the most trifling actions instead of often ascribing the greatest actions to the most trifling causes, in which they would be much seldomer mistaken. They read and write of kings, heroes, and statesmen as never doing anything but upon the deepest principles of sound policy.

But those who see and observe kings, heroes, and statesmen discover that they have headaches, indigestions, humors, and passions, just like other people, every one of which in their turns determine their wills in defiance of their reason. Had we only read in the Life of Alexander that he burnt Persepolis, it would doubtless have been accounted for from deep policy; we should have been told that his new conquest could not have been secured without the destruction of that capital which would have been the constant seat of cabals, conspiracies, and revolts. But luckily we are informed at the same time that this hero, this demi-god, this son and heir of Jupiter Ammon, happened to get extremely drunk with his mistress, and by way of frolic destroyed one of the finest cities in the world. Read men, therefore, yourself, not in books but in nature. Adopt no systems but study them yourself. Observe their weaknesses, their passions, their humors, of all which their understandings are nine times in ten the dupes. You will then know that they are to be gained, influenced, or led much oftener by little things than by great ones; and consequently you will no longer think those things little which tend to such great purposes.

Let us apply this now to the particular object of this letter,—I mean speaking in and influencing public assemblies. The nature of our constitution makes eloquence more useful and more necessary in this country than in any other in Europe. A certain degree of good sense and knowledge is requisite for that as well as for everything else; but beyond that, the purity of diction, the elegance of style, the harmony of periods, a pleasing elocution, and a graceful action are the things which a public speaker should attend to the most, because his audience certainly does, and understands them the best, or rather indeed understands little else. The late Lord Chancellor Cowper's strength as an orator lay by no means in his reasonings, for he often hazarded very weak ones. But such was the purity and elegance of his style, such the propriety and charms of his elocution, and such the gracefulness of his action, that he never spoke without universal applause; the ears and the eyes gave him up the hearts and the understandings of the audience. On the contrary, the late Lord Townshend always spoke materially, with argument and knowledge, but never pleased. Why? His diction was not only inelegant but frequently ungrammatical, always vulgar, his cadences false, his voice unharmonious, and his action ungraceful. Nobody heard him with patience, and the young fellows used to joke upon him and repeat his inaccuracies. The late Duke of Argyle,[1] though the weakest reasoner, was the most pleasing speaker I ever knew in my life; he charmed, he warmed, he forcibly ravished the audience, — not by his matter certainly, but by his manner of delivering it. A most genteel figure, a graceful, noble air, an harmonious voice, an elegance of style, and a strength of emphasis conspired

---

[1] Of whom Thomson wrote, —

—— " From his rich tongue
Persuasion flows and wins the high debate."

to make him the most affecting, persuasive, and applauded speaker I ever saw. I was captivated like others; but when I came home and coolly considered what he had said, stripped of all those ornaments in which he had dressed it, I often found the matter flimsy, the arguments weak, and I was convinced of the power of those adventitious concurring circumstances which ignorance of mankind only calls trifling ones. Cicero in his book *de Oratore*, in order to raise the dignity of that profession which he well knew himself to be at the head of, asserts that a complete orator must be a complete everything, lawyer, philosopher, divine, etc. That would be extremely well if it were possible, but man's life is not long enough; and I hold him to be the completest orator who speaks the best upon that subject which occurs, — whose happy choice of words, whose lively imagination, whose elocution and action adorn and grace his matter at the same time that they excite the attention and engage the passions of his audience.

You will be of the House of Commons as soon as you are of age; and you must first make a figure there, if you would make a figure or a fortune in your country. This you can never do without that correctness and elegance in your own language which you now seem to neglect and which you have entirely to learn. Fortunately for you, it is to be learned. Care and observation will do it; but do not flatter yourself that all the knowledge, sense, and reasoning in the world will ever make you a popular and applauded speaker without the ornaments and the graces of style, elocution, and action. Sense and argument, though coarsely delivered, will have their weight in a private conversation with two or three people of sense; but in a public assembly they will have none, if naked and destitute of the advantages I have mentioned. Cardinal de Retz observes very justly that every numerous assembly is a mob, influenced by their passions, humors, and affections, which nothing but eloquence ever did or ever can engage. This is so important a consideration for everybody in this country, and more particularly for you, that I earnestly recommend it to your most serious care and attention. Mind your diction in whatever language you either write or speak; contract a habit of correctness and elegance; consider your style even in the freest conversation and most familiar letters. After at least, if not before, you have said a thing, reflect if you could not have said it better. Where you doubt of the propriety or elegance of a word or a phrase, consult some good dead or living authority in that language. Use yourself to translate from various languages into English; correct those translations till they satisfy your ear as well as your understanding. And be convinced of this truth, that the best sense and reason in the world will be as unwelcome in a public assembly without these ornaments as they will in public companies without the assistance of manners and politeness. If you will please people you must please them in their own way; and as you cannot make them what they should be, you must take them as they are. I repeat it again, they are only to be taken by *agrémens* and by what flatters their senses and their hearts. Rabelais first wrote a most excellent book which nobody liked; then, determined to conform to the public taste, he wrote "Gargantua and Pantagruel," which everybody liked, extravagant as it was. Adieu.

XLIII.

"THE TONGUE TO PERSUADE."

LONDON, *Dec.* 12, O. S. 1749.

DEAR BOY, — Lord Clarendon in his history says of Mr. John Hampden that "he had a head to contrive, a tongue to persuade, and a hand to execute any mischief." I shall not now enter into the justness of this character of Mr. Hampden, to whose brave stand against the illegal demand of ship-money we owe our present liberties; but I mention it to you as the character, which, with the alteration of one single word, *Good*, instead of *Mischief*, I would have you aspire to, and use your utmost endeavors to deserve. The head to contrive God must to a certain degree have given you; but it is in your own power greatly to improve it by study, observation, and reflection. As for the "tongue to persuade," it wholly depends upon yourself; and without it the best head will contrive to very little purpose. The hand to execute depends likewise, in my opinion, in a great measure upon yourself. Serious reflection will always give courage in a good cause; and the courage arising from reflection is of a much superior nature to the animal and constitutional courage of a foot soldier. The former is steady and unshaken, where the *nodus* is *dignus vindice;* the latter is oftener improperly than properly exerted, but always brutally.

The second member of my text (to speak ecclesiastically) shall be the subject of my following discourse, — *the tongue to persuade*, — as judicious preachers recommend those virtues which they think their several audiences want the most, such as truth and continence at Court, disinterestedness in the city, and sobriety in the country.

You must certainly in the course of your little experience have felt the different effects of elegant and inelegant speaking. Do you not suffer when people accost you in a stammering or hesitating manner, in an untuneful voice with false accents and cadences, puzzling and blundering through solecisms, barbarisms, and vulgarisms, misplacing even their bad words, and inverting all method? Does not this prejudice you against their matter, be it what it will; nay, even against their persons? I am sure it does me. On the other hand, do you not feel yourself inclined, prepossessed, nay, even engaged in favor of those who address you in the direct contrary manner? The effects of a correct and adorned style, of method and perspicuity, are incredible towards persuasion; they often supply the want of reason and argument, but when used in the support of reason and argument, they are irresistible. The French attend very much to the purity and elegance of their style, even in common conversation; insomuch that it is a character to say of a man, "qu'il narre bien." Their conversations frequently turn upon the delicacies of their language, and an academy is employed in fixing it. The *Crusca* in Italy has the same object; and I have met with very few Italians who did not speak their own language correctly and elegantly. How much more necessary is it for an Englishman to do so, who is to speak it in a public assembly where the laws and liberties of his country are the subjects of his deliberation? The tongue that would persuade there must not content itself with mere articulation. . . . If you have the least defect in your elocution, take the utmost care and pains to correct it. Do not neglect your style, whatever language you speak in, or whomever you speak to, were it your footman. Seek always for the best words and the happiest expressions you can find. Do not content yourself with being barely understood, but adorn your thoughts, and dress them as you would your person; which, however well proportioned it might be, it would be very improper and indecent to exhibit naked, or even worse dressed than people of your sort are.

. . . .

XLIV.

MAN'S INCONSISTENCY. — RICHELIEU AND MAZARIN. — WOMEN MORE ALIKE THAN MEN. — ON RASH CONFIDENCES.

LONDON, *Dec.* 19, O. S. 1749.

DEAR BOY, — The knowledge of mankind is a very useful knowledge for everybody, — a most necessary one for you, who are destined to an active public life. You will have to do with all sorts of characters; you should therefore know them thoroughly in order to manage them ably. This knowledge is not to be gotten systematically; you must acquire it yourself by your own observation and sagacity. I will give you such hints as I think may be useful land-marks in your intended progress.

I have often told you (and it is most true) that with regard to mankind we must not draw general conclusions from certain particular principles, though in the main true ones. We must not suppose that because a man is a rational animal, he will therefore always act rationally; or because he has such or such a predominate passion, that he will act invariably and consequentially in the pursuit of it. No, we are complicated machines; and though we have one main spring that gives motion to the whole, we have an infinity of little wheels, which in their turns retard, precipitate, and sometimes stop that motion.

. . . .

There are two inconsistent passions, which however frequently accompany each other, like man and wife; and which, like man and wife too, are commonly clogs upon each other. I mean ambition and avarice. The latter is often the true cause of the former, and then is the predominant passion. It seems to have been so in Cardinal Mazarin, who did anything, submitted to anything, and forgave anything for the sake of plunder. He loved and courted power like an usurer, because it carried profit along with it. Whoever should have formed his opinion or taken his measures singly, from the ambitious part of Cardinal Mazarin's character, would have found himself often mistaken. Some who had found this out made their fortunes by letting him cheat them at play. On the contrary, Cardinal Richelieu's prevailing passion seems to have been ambition, and his immense riches only the natural consequences of that ambition gratified; and yet I make no doubt but that ambition had now and then its turn with the former, and avarice with the latter. Richelieu (by the way) is so strong a proof of the inconsistency of human nature that I cannot help observing to you that while he absolutely governed both his king and his country, and was in a great degree the arbiter of the fate of all Europe, he was more jealous of the great reputation of Corneille than of the power of Spain; and more flattered with being thought (what he was not) the best poet than with being thought (what he certainly was) the greatest statesman in Europe; and affairs stood still while he was concerting the criticism upon the "Cid." Could one think this possible if one did not know it to be true? Though men are all of one composition, the several ingredients are so differently proportioned in each individual, that no two are exactly alike, and no one at all times like himself. The ablest man will sometimes do weak things; the proudest man, mean things; the honestest man, ill things; and the wickedest man, good ones. Study individuals then, and if you take (as you ought to do) their outlines from their prevailing passion, suspend your last finishing strokes till you have attended to and discovered the operations of their inferior passions, appetites, and humors. A man's general character may be that of the honestest man of the world. Do not dispute it, — you might be thought envious or ill-natured; but at the same time do not take this probity upon trust to such a degree as to put your life, fortune, or reputation in his power. This honest man may happen to be your rival in power, in interest, or in love, — three passions that often put honesty to most severe trials in which it is too often cast; but first analyze this honest man yourself, and then only you will be able to judge how far you may, or may not, with safety trust him.

Women are much more like each other than men: they have in truth but two passions, vanity and love; these are their universal characteristics. An Agrippina may sacrifice them to ambition, or a Messalina to lust, but those instances are rare; and in general all they say and all they do, tends to the gratification of their vanity or their love. He who flatters them most pleases them best, and they are the most in love with him who they think is the most in love with them. No adulation is too strong for them; no assiduity too great; as, on the other hand, the least word or action that can possibly be construed into a slight or contempt is unpardonable, and never forgotton. Men are in this respect tender too, and will sooner forgive an injury than an insult. Some men are more captious than others; some are always wrong-headed; but every man living has such a share of vanity as to be hurt by marks of slight and contempt. Every man does not pretend to be a poet, a mathematician, or a statesman, and considered as such; but every man pretends to common-sense and to fill his place in the world with common decency, and consequently does not easily forgive those negligences, inattentions, and slights which seem to call in question or utterly deny him both these pretensions.

Suspect, in general, those who remarkably affect any one virtue; who raise it above all others, and who in a manner intimate that they possess it exclusively. I say suspect them, for they are commonly impostors; but do not be sure that they are always so, for I have sometimes known saints really religious, blusterers really brave, reformers of manners really honest, and prudes really chaste. Pry into the recesses of their hearts yourself, as far as you are able, and never implicitly adopt a character upon common fame, — which though generally right as to the great outlines of characters is always wrong in some particulars.

Be upon your guard against those who upon very slight acquaintance obtrude their unasked and unmerited friendship and confidence upon you, for they probably cram you with them only for their own eating; but at the same time, do not roughly reject them upon that general supposition. Examine further and see whether those unexpected offers flow from a warm heart and a silly head, or from a designing head and a cold heart; for knavery and folly have often the same symptoms. In the first case there is no danger in accepting them, *Valeant quantum valere possunt.* In the latter case it may be useful to seem to accept them, and artfully to turn the battery upon him who raised it.

There is an incontinency of friendship among young fellows who are associated by their mutual pleasures only, which has very frequently bad consequences. A parcel of warm hearts and inexperienced heads, heated by convivial mirth and possibly a little too much wine, vow, and really mean at the time, eternal friendships to each other, and indiscreetly pour out their whole souls in common, and without the least reserve. These confidences are as indiscreetly repealed as they were made; for new pleasures and new places soon dissolve this ill-cemented connection; and then very ill uses are made of these rash confidences. Bear your part, however, in young companies; nay, excel if you can in all the social and convivial joy and festivity that become youth, — but keep your serious views secret. Trust those only to some tried friend, more experienced than yourself, and who being in a different walk of life from you, is not likely to become your rival; for I would not advise you to depend so much upon the heroic virtue of mankind as to hope or believe that your competitor will ever be your friend as to the object of that competition.

These are reserves and cautions very necessary to have, but very imprudent to show; the *volto sciolto* should accompany them. Adieu.

XLV.

ON THE *LENIORES VIRTUTES.*

[*No Date.*]

DEAR BOY,—Great talents and great virtues (if you should have them) will procure you the respect and the admiration of mankind; but it is the lesser talents, the *leniores virtutes*, which must procure you their love and affection. The former, unassisted and unadorned by the latter, will extort praise, but will at the same time excite both fear and envy,— two sentiments absolutely incompatible with love and affection.

Caesar had all the great vices and Cato all the great virtues that men could have. But Caesar had the *leniores virtutes*, which Cato wanted, and which made him beloved even by his enemies and gained him the hearts of mankind in spite of their reason; while Cato was not even beloved by his friends, notwithstanding the esteem and respect which they could not refuse to his virtues; and I am apt to think that if Caesar had wanted and Cato possessed those *leniores virtutes*, the former would not have attempted (at least with success) and the latter could have protected the liberties of Rome. Mr. Addison, in his Cato, says of Caesar,— and I believe with truth, —

"Curse on his virtues, they've undone his country!"

By which he means those lesser but engaging virtues of gentleness, affability, complaisance, and good humor. The knowledge of a scholar, the courage of a hero, and the virtue of a Stoic, will be admired; but if the knowledge be accompanied with arrogance, the courage with ferocity, and the virtue with inflexible severity, the man will never be loved. The heroism of Charles XII. of Sweden (if his brutal courage deserves that name) was universally admired, but the man nowhere beloved; whereas Henry IV. of France, who had full as much courage and was much longer engaged in wars, was generally beloved upon account of his lesser and social virtues. We are all so formed that our understandings are generally the dupes of our hearts, that is, of our passions; and the surest way to the former is through the latter, which must be engaged by the *leniores virtutes* alone and the manner of exerting them. The insolent civility of a proud man is, for example, if possible more shocking than his rudeness could be, because he shows you by his manner that he thinks it mere condescension in him; and that his goodness alone bestows upon you what you have no pretence to claim. He intimates his protection instead of his friendship by a gracious nod instead of an usual bow; and rather signifies his consent that you may, than his invitation that you should, sit, walk, eat, or drink with him.

The costive liberality of a purse-proud man insults the distresses it sometimes relieves; he takes care to make you feel your own misfortunes and the difference between your situation and his, — both which he insinuates to be justly merited, yours by your folly, his by his wisdom. The arrogant pedant does not communicate but promulgates his knowledge. He does not give it you but he inflicts it upon you; and is (if possible) more desirous to show you your own ignorance than his own learning. Such manners as these not only in the particular instances which I have mentioned, but likewise in all others, shock and revolt that little pride and vanity which every man has in his heart, and obliterate in us the obligation for the favor conferred by reminding us of the motive which produced and the manner which accompanied it.

These faults point out their opposite perfections, and your own good sense will naturally suggest them to you.

But besides these lesser virtues, there are what may be called the lesser talents, or accomplishments, which are of great use to adorn and recommend all the greater; and the more so as all people are judges of the one and but few are of the other. Everybody feels the impression which an engaging address, an agreeable manner of speaking, and an easy politeness makes upon them; and they prepare the way for the favorable reception of their betters. Adieu.

XLVI.

THE WRITER'S NOVITIATE.

LONDON, *Jan.* 11, O. S. 1750.

MY DEAR FRIEND,[1] —Yesterday I received a letter from Mr. Harte of the 31st December, N. S., which

[1] Lord Chesterfield uses this form of address in all the subsequent letters to his son.

I will answer soon, and for which I desire you to return him my thanks now. He tells me two things that give me great satisfaction: one is, that there are very few English at Rome; the other is, that you frequent the best foreign companies. This last is a very good symptom; for a man of sense is never desirous to frequent those companies where he is not desirous to please or where he finds that he displeases. It will not be expected in those companies that at your age you should have the *garbo*, the *disinvoltura*, and the *leggiadria* of a man of five and twenty who has been long used to keep the best companies; and therefore do not be discouraged and think yourself either slighted or laughed at, because you see others older and more used to the world easier, more familiar, and consequently rather better received in those companies than yourself. In time your turn will come; and if you do but show an inclination, a desire to please, though you should be embarrassed or even err in the means which must necessarily happen to you at first, yet the will — to use a vulgar expression — will be taken for the deed; and people instead of laughing at you will be glad to instruct you. Good sense can only give you the great outlines of good breeding, but observation and usage can alone give you the delicate touches and the fine coloring. You will naturally endeavor to show the utmost respect to people of certain ranks and characters, and consequently you will show it; but the proper, the delicate manner of showing that respect nothing but observation and time can give.

I remember that when with all the awkwardness and rust of Cambridge about me, I was first introduced into good company, I was frightened out of my wits. I was determined to be what I thought civil; I made fine low bows and placed myself below everybody; but when I was spoken to or attempted to speak myself, *Obstupui, steteruntque comae et vox faucibus haesit.* If I saw people whisper, I was sure it was at me; and I thought myself the sole object of either the ridicule or the censure of the whole company, who God knows did not trouble their heads about me. In this way I suffered for some time like a criminal at the bar, and should certainly have renounced all polite company forever if I had not been so convinced of the absolute necessity of forming my manners upon those of the best companies that I determined to persevere, and suffer anything or everything rather than not compass that point. Insensibly it grew easier to me, and I began not to bow so ridiculously low and to answer questions without great hesitation or stammering; if now and then some charitable people seeing my embarrassment and being *desœuvré* themselves came and spoke to me, I considered them as angels sent to comfort me, and that gave me a little courage. I got more soon afterwards and was intrepid enough to go up to a fine woman and tell her that I thought it a warm day. She answered me very civilly that she thought so too; upon which the conversation ceased on my part for some time, till she good-naturedly resuming it spoke to me thus: "I see your embarrassment, and I am sure that the few words you said to me cost you a great deal; but do not be discouraged for that reason and avoid good company. We see that you desire to please, and that is the main point; you want only the manner, and you think that you want it still more than you do. You must go through your novitiate before you can profess good breeding; and if you will be my novice I will present you to my acquaintance as such."

You will easily imagine how much this speech pleased me and how awkwardly I answered it. I hemmed once or twice (for it gave me a burr in my throat) before I could tell her that I was very much obliged to her; that it was true that I had a great deal of reason to distrust my own behavior, not being used to fine company; and that I should be proud of being her novice and receiving her instructions.

As soon as I had fumbled out this answer, she called up three or four people to her and said, " Do you know that I have undertaken this young man and that he must be encouraged? As for me I think I have made a conquest of him, for he just now ventured to tell me, although tremblingly, that it is warm. You will assist me in polishing him.". . .

The company laughed at this lecture, and I was stunned with it. I did not know whether she was serious or in jest. By turns I was pleased, ashamed, encouraged, and dejected. But when I found afterwards that both she and those to whom she had presented me countenanced and protected me in company, I gradually got more assurance, and began not to be ashamed of endeavoring to be civil. I copied the best masters, at first servilely, afterwards more freely, and at last I joined habit and invention.

. . . .

XLVII.

TO ACQUIRE THE GRACES AND ACCOMPLISHMENTS, STUDY THE BEST MODELS. — A LIST OF THE GRACES.

LONDON, *Jan.* 18, O. S. 1750.

MY DEAR FRIEND, — I consider the solid part of your little edifice as so near being finished and completed that my only remaining care is about the embellishments; and that must now be your principal care too. Adorn yourself with all those graces and accomplishments which without solidity are frivolous, but without which solidity is to a great degree useless. Take one man with a very moderate degree of knowledge, but with a pleasing figure, a prepossessing address, graceful in all that he says and does, polite, *liant*, and in short, adorned with all the lesser talents; and take another man, with sound sense and profound knowledge, but without the above-mentioned advantages: the former will not only get the better of the latter in every pursuit of every kind, but in truth there will be no sort of competition between them. But can every man acquire these advantages? I say, Yes, if he please; suppose he is in a situation and in circumstances to frequent good company. Attention, observation, and imitation will most infallibly do it. When you see a man whose first *abord* strikes you, prepossesses you in his favor, and makes you entertain a good opinion of him, you do not know why, analyze that *abord* and examine within yourself the several parts that compose it, and you will generally find it to be the result, the happy assemblage, of modesty unembarrassed, respect without timidity, a genteel but unaffected attitude of body and limbs, an open, cheerful, but unsmirking countenance, and a dress by no means negligent, and yet not foppish. Copy him then not servilely, but as some of the greatest masters of painting have copied others, — insomuch that their copies have been equal to the originals both as to beauty and freedom. When you see a man who is universally allowed to shine as an agreeable well-bred man, and a fine gentleman (as for example, the Duke de Nivernois), attend to him, watch him carefully; observe in what manner he addresses himself to his superiors, how he lives with his equals, and how he treats his inferiors. Mind his turn of conversation in the several situations of morning visits, the table, and the evening amusements. Imitate without mimicking him; and be his duplicate, but not his ape. You will find that he takes care never to say or do anything that can be construed into a slight or a negligence, or that can in any degree mortify people's vanity and self-love; on the contrary you will perceive that he makes people pleased with him by making them first pleased with themselves; he shows respect, regard, esteem, and attention, where they are severally proper; he sows them with care, and he reaps them in plenty.

These amiable accomplishments are all to be acquired by use and imitation; for we are in truth more than half what we are by imitation. The great point is to choose good models, and to study them with care. People insensibly contract not only the air, the manners, and the vices, of those with whom they commonly converse, but their virtues too, and even their way of thinking. This is so true that I have known very plain understandings catch a certain degree of wit by constantly conversing with those who had a great deal. Persist therefore in keeping the best company, and you will insensibly become like them; but if you add attention and observation, you will very soon become one of them. The inevitable contagion of company shows you the necessity of keeping the best and avoiding all other; for in every one something will stick. You have hitherto, I confess, had very few opportunities of keeping polite company. Westminster school is undoubtedly the seat of illiberal manners and brutal behavior; Leipsig, I suppose, is not the seat of refined and elegant manners; Venice, I believe, has done something; Rome, I hope, will do a great deal more; and Paris will, I dare say, do all that you want, — always supposing that you frequent the best companies and in the intention of improving and forming yourself, for without that intention nothing will do.

I here subjoin a list of all those necessary ornamental accomplishments (without which no man living can either please or rise in the world) which hitherto I fear you want, and which only require your care and attention to possess, —

To speak elegantly whatever language you speak in, without which nobody will hear you with pleasure, and consequently you will speak to very little purpose.

An agreeable and distinct elocution, without which nobody will hear you with patience. This everybody may acquire, who is not born with some imperfection in the organs of speech. You are not, and therefore it is wholly in your power. You need take much less pains for it than Demosthenes did.

A distinguished politeness of manners and address, which common-sense, observation, good company, and imitation will infallibly give you if you will accept it.

A genteel carriage and graceful motions, with the air of a man of fashion. A good dancing-master, with some care on your part and some imitation of those who excel, will soon bring this about.

To be extremely clean in your person, and perfectly well dressed, according to the fashion, be that what it will. Your negligence of your dress while you were a school-boy was pardonable, but would not be so now.

Upon the whole, take it for granted that without these accomplishments all you know and all you can do will avail you very little. Adieu.

XLVIII.

IMPORTANCE OF THE MORAL VIRTUES. — WARNING AGAINST VANITY.

LONDON, *May* 17, O. S. 1750.

MY DEAR FRIEND, — Your apprenticeship is near out, and you are soon to set up for yourself; that approaching moment is a critical one for you, and an anxious one for me. A tradesman who would succeed in his way must begin by establishing a character of integrity and good manners: without the former, nobody will go to his shop at all; without the latter, nobody will go there twice. This rule does not exclude the fair arts of trade. He may sell his goods at the best price he can, within certain bounds. He may avail himself of the humor, the whims, and the fantastical tastes of his customers; but what he warrants to be good must be really so, what he seriously asserts must be true, or his first fraudulent profits will soon end in a bankruptcy. It is the same in higher life and in the great business of the world. A man who does not solidly establish, and really deserve, a character of truth, probity, good manners, and good morals at his first setting out in the world, may impose and shine like a meteor for a very short time, but will very soon vanish, and be extinguished with contempt. People easily pardon in young men the common irregularities of the senses; but they do not forgive the least vice of the heart. The heart never grows better by age; I fear rather worse; always harder. A young liar will be an old one, and a young knave will only be a greater knave as he grows older. But should a bad young heart, accompanied with a good head (which by the way very seldom is the case), really reform in a more advanced age, from a consciousness of its folly, as well as of its guilt, such a conversion would only be thought prudential and political, but never sincere. I hope in God, and I verily believe, that you want no moral virtue. But the possession of all the moral virtues *in actu primo*, as the logicians call it, is not sufficient; you must have them *in actu secundo* too; nay, that is not sufficient neither, you must have the reputation of them also. Your character in the world must be built upon that solid foundation, or it will soon fall, and upon your own head. You cannot therefore be too careful, too nice, too scrupulous, in establishing this character at first, upon which your whole career depends. Let no conversation, no example, no fashion, no *bon mot*, no silly desire of seeming to be above what most knaves and many fools call prejudices, ever tempt you to avow, excuse, extenuate, or laugh at the least breach of morality; but show upon all occasions, and take all occasions to show, a detestation and abhorrence of it. There, though young, you ought to be strict; and there only, while young, it becomes you to be strict and severe. But there too, spare the persons while you lash the crimes. All this relates, as you easily judge, to the vices of the heart, such as lying, fraud, envy, malice, detraction, etc., and I do not extend it to the little frailties of youth flowing from high spirits and warm blood. It would ill become you at your age to declaim against them, and sententiously censure an accidental excess of the table, a frolic, an inadvertency; no, keep as free from them yourself as you can, but say nothing against them in others. They certainly mend by time, often by reason; and a man's worldly character is not affected by them, provided it be pure in all other respects.

To come now to a point of much less but yet of very great consequence at your first setting out. Be extremely upon your guard against vanity, the common failing of inexperienced youth; but particularly against that kind of vanity that dubs a man a coxcomb, — a character which, once acquired, is more indelible than that of the priesthood. It is not to be imagined by how many different ways vanity defeats its own purposes. Some men decide peremptorily upon every subject, betray their ignorance upon many, and show a disgusting presumption upon the rest.... Others flatter their vanity by little extraneous objects, which have not the least relation to themselves, — such as being descended from, related to, or acquainted with people of distinguished merit and eminent characters. They talk perpetually of their grandfather such-a-one, their uncle such-a-one and their intimate friend Mr. Such-a-one, with whom possibly they are hardly acquainted. But admitting it all to be as they would have it, what then? Have they the more merit for those accidents? Certainly not. On the contrary, their taking up adventitious proves their want of intrinsic merit; a rich man never borrows. Take this rule for granted, as a never-failing one, — that you must never seem to affect the character in which you have a mind to shine. Modesty is the only sure bait when you angle for praise. The affectation of courage will make even a brave man pass only for a bully, as the affectation of wit will make a man of parts pass for a coxcomb. By this modesty I do not mean timidity and awkward bashfulness. On the contrary, be inwardly firm and steady, know your own value whatever it may be, and act upon that principle; but take great care to let nobody discover that you do know your own value. Whatever real merit you have, other people will discover, and people always magnify their own discoveries, as they lessen those of others.

. . . .

XLIX.

HOW TO READ HISTORY, AND HOW TO CONVERSE WITH ADVANTAGE.— A MODEST ASSURANCE.

LONDON, *Nov.* 1, O. S. 1750.

MY DEAR FRIEND, — . . . While you are in France, I could wish that the hours you allot for historical amusement should be entirely devoted to the history of France. One always reads history to most advantage in that country to which it is relative, — not only books but persons being ever at hand to solve doubts and clear up difficulties. I do by no means advise you to throw away your time in ransacking, like a dull antiquarian, the minute and unimportant parts of remote and fabulous times. Let blockheads read what blockheads wrote.

. . . .

Conversation in France, if you have the address and dexterity to turn it upon useful subjects, will exceedingly improve your historical knowledge, for people there, however classically ignorant they may be, think it a shame to be ignorant of the history of their own country; they read that, if they read nothing else, and having often read nothing else are proud of having read that, and talk of it willingly; even the women are well instructed in that sort of reading. I am far from meaning by this that you should always be talking wisely in company of books, history, and matters of knowledge. There are many companies which you will and ought to keep, where such conversations would be misplaced and ill-timed. Your own good sense must distinguish the company and the time. You must trifle only with triflers and be serious only with the serious, but dance to those who pipe. " Cur in theatrum Cato severe venisti? " was justly said to an old man; how much more so would it be to one of your age! From the moment that you are dressed and go out, pocket all your knowledge with your watch, and never pull it out in company unless desired; the producing of the one unasked implies that you are weary of the company, and the producing of the other unrequired will make the company weary of you. Company is a republic too jealous of its liberties to suffer a dictator even for a quarter of an hour, and yet in that, as in all republics, there are some few who really govern; but then it is by seeming to disclaim, instead of attempting to usurp the power. That is the occasion in which manners, dexterity, address, and the undefinable *je ne sais quoi* triumph; if properly exerted their conquest is sure, and the more lasting for not being perceived. Remember that this is not only your first and greatest, but ought to be almost your only object, while you are in France.

I know that many of your countrymen are apt to call the freedom and vivacity of the French petulancy and ill breeding; but should you think so, I desire upon many accounts that you will not say so. I admit that it may be so in some instances of *petits maîtres étourdis*, and in some young people unbroken to the world; but I can assure you that you will find it much otherwise with people of a certain rank and age, upon whose model you will do very well to form yourself. We call their steady assurance, impudence. Why? Only because what we call modesty is awkward bashfulness and *mauvaise honte*. For my part I see no impudence, but on the contrary infinite utility and advantage, in presenting one's self with the same coolness and unconcern in any and every company; till one can do that, I am very sure that one can never present one's self well. Whatever is done under concern and embarrassment, must be ill done; and till a man is absolutely easy and unconcerned in every company he will never be thought to have kept good, nor be very welcome in it. A steady assurance with seeming modesty is possibly the most useful qualification that a man can have in every part of life. A man would certainly make a very considerable fortune and figure in the world, whose modesty and timidity should often, as bashfulness always does, put him in the deplorable and lamentable situation of the pious Æneas, when *obstupuit, steteruntque comæ, et vox faucibus hæsit*. Fortune,

"——— born to be controlled,
Stoops to the forward and the bold."

Assurance and intrepidity, under the white banner of seeming modesty, clear the way for merit, that would otherwise be discouraged by difficulties in its journey; whereas barefaced impudence is the noisy and blustering harbinger of a worthless and senseless usurper.

You will think that I shall never have done recommending to you these exterior worldly accomplishments, and you will think right, for I never shall. They are of too great consequence to you for me to be indifferent or negligent about them; the shining part of your future figure and fortune depends now wholly upon them. These are the acquisitions which must give efficacy and success to those you have already made. To have it said and believed that you are the most learned man in England would be no more than was said and believed of Dr. Bentley; but to have it said at the same time that you are also the best bred, most polite, and agreeable man in the kingdom, would be such a happy composition of a character as I never yet knew any one man deserve, and which I will endeavor as well as ardently wish that you may. Absolute perfection is I well know unattainable; but I know too that a man of parts may be unweariedly aiming at it, and arrive pretty near it. Try, labor, persevere. Adieu.

L.

GOOD MANNERS THE SOURCE OF ESTEEM.— SUPPOSED ALLUSION TO DR. JOHNSON.

LONDON, *Feb.* 28, O. S. 1751.

MY DEAR FRIEND, — This epigram in Martial,

Non amo te, Sabidi, nec possum dicere quare,
Hoc tantum possum dicere, non amo te;[1]

has puzzled a great many people who cannot conceive how it is possible not to love anybody and yet not to know the reason why. I think I conceive Martial's meaning very clearly, though the nature of epigram, which is to be short, would not allow him to explain it more fully; and I take it to be this: O Sabidis, you are a very worthy, deserving man; you have a thousand good qualities, you have a great deal of learning; I esteem, I respect, but for the soul of me I cannot love you, though I cannot particularly say why. You are not *aimable;* you have not those engaging manners, those pleasing attentions, those graces, and that address, which

[1] Recalling, —

"I do not love thee, Dr. Fell, the reason why I cannot tell,
But this I know and know full well, I do not love thee, Dr. Fell."

are absolutely necessary to please though impossible to define. I cannot say it is this or that particular thing that hinders me from loving you, — it is the whole together; and upon the whole you are not agreeable.

How often have I in the course of my life found myself in this situation with regard to many of my acquaintance whom I have honored and respected without being able to love. I did not know why, because when one is young one does not take the trouble nor allow one's self the time to analyze one's sentiments and to trace them up to their source. But subsequent observation and reflection have taught me why. There is a man whose moral character, deep learning, and superior parts, I acknowledge, admire, and respect; but whom it is so impossible for me to love, that I am almost in a fever whenever I am in his company. His figure (without being deformed) seems made to disgrace or ridicule the common structure of the human body. His legs and arms are never in the position which according to the situation of his body they ought to be in, but constantly employed in committing acts of hostility upon the Graces. He throws anywhere but down his throat whatever he means to drink, and only mangles what he means to carve. Inattentive to all the regards of social life, he mis-times or misplaces everything. He disputes with heat, and indiscriminately, mindless of the rank, character, and situation of those with whom he disputes; absolutely ignorant of the several gradations of familiarity or respect, he is exactly the same to his superiors, his equals, and his inferiors, and therefore, by a necessary consequence absurd to two of the three. Is it possible to love such a man? No. The utmost I can do for him is to consider him as a respectable Hottentot.[1]

. . . .

LI.

SUAVITER IN MODO, FORTITER IN RE.

[*No Date*].

MY DEAR FRIEND, — I mentioned to you some time ago, a sentence, which I would most earnestly wish you always to retain in your thoughts and observe in your conduct. It is *Suaviter in modo, fortiter in re.* I do not know any one rule so unexceptionably useful and necessary in every part of life. I shall therefore take it for my text to-day; and as old men love preaching, and I have some right to preach to you, I here present you with my sermon upon these words. To proceed then regularly and *pulpitically*, I will first show you, my

[1] Lord Chesterfield probably alludes to Dr. Johnson in this passage. Boswell had no doubt of it, and says: — " I have heard Johnson himself talk of the character, and say that it was meant for Lord George Lyttelton, in which I could by no means agree; for his Lordship had nothing of that violence which is a conspicuous feature in the composition. Finding that my illustrious friend could bear to have it supposed that it might be meant for him, I said laughingly that there was one *trait* which did not belong to him, — *he throws meat everywhere but down his own throat.* 'Sir,' said he, ' Lord Chesterfield never saw me eat in his life!' "

beloved, the necessary connection of the two members of my text, — *suaviter in modo ; fortiter in re.* In the next place, I shall set forth the advantages and utility resulting from a strict observance of the precept contained in my text; and conclude with an application of the whole. The *suaviter in modo* alone would degenerate and sink into a mean, timid complaisance and passiveness, if not supported and dignified by the *fortiter in re*, which would also run into impetuosity and brutality, if not tempered and softened by the *suaviter in modo ;* however, they are seldom united. The warm, choleric man with strong animal spirits despises the *suaviter in modo*, and thinks to carry all before him by the *fortiter in re*. He may possibly, by great accident, now and then succeed, when he has only weak and timid people to deal with; but his general fate will be to shock, offend, be hated, and fail. On the other hand, the cunning, crafty man thinks to gain all his ends by the *suaviter in modo* only; *he becomes all things to all men ;* he seems to have no opinion of his own, and servilely adopts the present opinion of the present person; he insinuates himself only into the esteem of fools, but is soon detected, and surely despised by everybody else. The wise man (who differs as much from the cunning as from the choleric man) alone joins the *suaviter in modo* with the *fortiter in re*. Now to the advantages arising from the strict observance of this precept. If you are in authority and have a right to command, your commands delivered *suaviter in modo* will be willingly, cheerfully, and consequently well obeyed; whereas, if given only *fortiter*, that is brutally, they will rather, as Tacitus says, be interrupted than executed. For my own part, if I bid my footman bring me a glass of wine in a rough insulting manner, I should expect that in obeying me he would contrive to spill some of it upon me, and I am sure I should deserve it. A cool, steady resolution should show that where you have a right to command you will be obeyed, but at the same time a gentleness in the manner of enforcing that obedience should make it a cheerful one, and soften as much as possible the mortifying consciousness of inferiority. If you are to ask a favor or even to solicit your due you must do it *suaviter in modo* or you will give those who have a mind to refuse you either, a pretence to do it by resenting the manner; but on the other hand you must by a steady perseverance and decent tenaciousness show the *fortiter in re*. The right motives are seldom the true ones of men's actions, — especially of kings, ministers, and people in high stations, who often give to importunity and fear what they would refuse to justice or to merit. By the *suaviter in modo* engage their hearts if you can; at least prevent the pretence of offence: but take care to show enough of the *fortiter in re* to extort from their love of ease or their fear what you might in vain hope for from their justice or good nature. People in high life are hardened to the wants and distresses of mankind as surgeons are to their bodily pains; they see and hear of them all day long and even of so many simulated ones that they do not know which are real and which not. Other sentiments are therefore to be applied to than those of mere justice and humanity. Their favor must be captivated by the *suaviter in modo*; their love of ease disturbed by unwearied importunity; or their fears wrought upon by a decent intimation of implacable cool resentment, — this is the true *fortiter in re*. This precept is the only way I know in the world of being loved without being despised and feared without being hated. It constitutes the dignity of character which every wise man must endeavor to establish.

Now to apply what has been said and so conclude.

If you find that you have a hastiness in your temper which unguardedly breaks out into indiscreet sallies or rough expressions to either your superiors, your equals, or your inferiors, watch it narrowly, check it carefully, and call the *suaviter in modo* to your assistance; at the first impulse of passion, be silent till you can be soft. Labor even to get the command of your countenance so well that those emotions may not be read in it, — a most unspeakable advantage in business. On the other hand, let no complaisance, no gentleness of temper, no weak desire of pleasing on your part, no wheedling, coaxing, nor flattery on other people's, make you recede one jot from any point that reason and prudence have bid you pursue; but return to the charge, persist, persevere, and you will find most things attainable that are possible. A yielding, timid meekness is always abused and insulted by the unjust and the unfeeling, but when sustained by the *fortiter in re* is always respected, commonly successful. In your friendships and connections, as well as in your enmities, this rule is particularly useful: let your firmness and vigor preserve and invite attachments to you, but at the same time let your manner hinder the enemies of your friends and dependants from becoming yours; let your enemies be disarmed by the gentleness of your manner, but let them feel at the same time the steadiness of your just resentment, — for there is a great difference between bearing malice, which is always ungenerous, and a resolute self-defence, which is always prudent and justifiable. In negotiations with foreign ministers remember the *fortiter in re;* give up no point, accept of no expedient, till the utmost necessity reduces you to it, and even then dispute the ground inch by inch; but then while you are contending with the minister *fortiter in re*, remember to gain the man by the *suaviter in modo*. If you engage his heart, you have a fair chance for imposing upon his understanding and determining his will. Tell him in a frank gallant manner that your ministerial wrangles do not lessen your personal regard for his merit, but that on the contrary his zeal and ability in the service of his master increase it, and that of all things you desire to make a good friend of so good a servant. By these means you may and will very often be a gainer; you never can be a loser. Some people cannot gain upon themselves to be easy and civil to those who are either their rivals, competitors, or opposers, though, independently of those accidental circumstances, they would like and esteem them. They betray a shyness and an awkwardness in company with them and catch at any little thing to expose them, and so from temporary and only occasional opponents make them their personal enemies. This is exceedingly weak and detrimental, as indeed is all humor in business, which can only be carried on successfully by unadulterated good policy and right reasoning. In such situations I would be more particularly and *noblement* civil, easy, and frank with the man whose designs I traversed. This is commonly called generosity and magnanimity but is in truth good sense and policy. The manner is often as important as the matter, sometimes more so. A favor may make an enemy and an injury may make a friend according to the different manner in which they are severally done. The countenance, the address, the words, the enunciation, the Graces add great efficacy to the *suaviter in modo* and great dignity to the *fortiter in re;* and consequently they deserve the utmost attention.

From what has been said, I conclude with this observation, — that gentleness of manners with firmness of mind is a short but full description of human perfection on this side of religious and moral duties. That you may be seriously convinced of this truth and show it in your life and conversation, is the most sincere and ardent wish of,

Yours.

LII.

LES BIENSÉANCES.—THE PROPER DEMEANOR WITH ONE'S SUPERIORS, IN MIXED COMPANIES, AND WITH ONE'S INFERIORS.

GREENWICH, *June* 13, O. S. 1751.

MY DEAR FRIEND,— *Les bienséances* [1] are a most necessary part of the knowledge of the world. They consist in the relations of persons, things, time, and place; good sense points them out, good company perfects them (supposing always an attention and a desire to please), and good policy recommends them.

Were you to converse with a king, you ought to be as easy and unembarrassed as with your own *valet de chambre*; but yet, every look, word, and action should imply the utmost respect. What would be proper and well bred with others much your superiors would be absurd and ill bred with one so very much so. You must wait till you are spoken to; you must receive not give the subject of conversation; and you must even take care that the given subject of such conversation do not lead you into any impropriety. The art would be to carry it, if possible, to some indirect flattery,— such as commending those virtues in some other person in which that prince either thinks he does, or at least would be thought by others to excel. Almost the same precautions are necessary to be used with ministers, generals, etc., who expect to be treated

[1] Good breeding; decorum; propriety.

with very near the same respect as their masters, and commonly deserve it better. There is, however, this difference, that one may begin the conversation with them, if on their side it should happen to drop, provided one does not carry it to any subject upon which it is improper either for them to speak or be spoken to. In these two cases certain attitudes and actions would be extremely absurd, because too easy and consequently disrespectful. As for instance if you were to put your arms across in your bosom, twirl your snuff-box, trample with your feet, scratch your head, etc., it would be shockingly ill bred in that company; and indeed not extremely well bred in any other. The great difficulty in those cases, though a very surmountable one by attention and custom, is to join perfect inward ease with perfect outward respect.

In mixed companies with your equals (for in mixed companies all people are to a certain degree equal), greater ease and liberty are allowed; but they too have their bounds within *bienséance*. There is a social respect necessary: you may start your own subject of conversation with modesty, taking great care, however, "de ne jamais parler de cordes dans la maison d'un pendu."[1] Your words, gestures, and attitudes have a greater degree of latitude, though by no means an unbounded one. You may have your hands in your pockets, take snuff, sit, stand, or occasionally walk, as you like; but I believe you would not think it very *bienséant* to

[1] Never to mention a rope in the family of a man who has been hanged.

whistle, put on your hat, loosen your garters or your buckles, lie down upon a couch, or go to bed, and welter in an easy-chair. These are negligences and freedoms which one can only take when quite alone; they are injurious to superiors, shocking and offensive to equals, brutal and insulting to inferiors. That easiness of carriage and behavior which is exceedingly engaging widely differs from negligence and inattention, and by no means implies that one may do whatever one pleases, — it only means that one is not to be stiff, formal, embarrassed, disconcerted, and ashamed, like country bumpkins and people who have never been in good company; but it requires great attention to and a scrupulous observation of *les bienséances*. Whatever one ought to do is to be done with ease and unconcern; whatever is improper must not be done at all. In mixed companies also, different ages and sexes are to be differently addressed. You would not talk of your pleasures to men of a certain age, gravity, and dignity; they justly expect from young people a degree of deference and regard. You should be full as easy with them as with people of your own years, but your manner must be different; more respect must be implied; and it is not amiss to insinuate that from them you expect to learn. It flatters and comforts age for not being able to take a part in the joy and titter of youth. To women you should always address yourself with great outward respect and attention, whatever you feel inwardly. Their sex is by long prescription entitled to it; and it is among the duties of *bienséance*. At the same time that respect is very properly and very agreeably mixed with a degree of *enjouement* if you have it: but then, that *badinage* must either directly or indirectly tend to their praise, and even not be liable to a malicious construction to their disadvantage. But here, too, great attention must be had to the difference of age, rank, and situation. A *Maréchale* of fifty must not be played with like a young coquette of fifteen; respect and *serious enjouement*, if I may couple those two words, must be used with the former, and mere *badinage, zesté même d'un peu de polissonerie* is pardonable with the latter.

Another important point of *les bienséances*, seldom enough attended to, is not to run your own present humor and disposition indiscriminately against everybody; but to observe, conform to, and adopt theirs. For example, if you happened to be in high good-humor and a flow of spirits, would you go and sing a *pont neuf*[1] or cut a caper to la Maréchale de Coigny, the Pope's Nuncio, or Abbé Sallier, or to any person of natural gravity and melancholy, or who at that time should be in grief? I believe not; as on the other hand, I suppose that if you were in low spirits or real grief, you would not choose to bewail your situation with *la petite Blot*. If you cannot command your present humor and disposition, single out those to converse with who happen to be in the humor the nearest to your own.

Loud laughter is extremely inconsistent with *les bienséances*, as it is only the illiberal and noisy testi-

[1] Ballad.

mony of the joy of the mob at some very silly thing. A gentleman is often seen but very seldom heard to laugh. Nothing is more contrary to *les bienséances* than horse-play, or *jeux de main* of any kind whatever, and has often very serious, sometimes very fatal consequences. Romping, struggling, throwing things at one another's head, are the becoming pleasantries of the mob, but degrade a gentleman; *Giuoco di mano, giuoco di villano* is a very true saying, among the few true sayings of the Italians.

Peremptoriness and decision in young people is *contraire aux bienséances*, and they should seldom seem to assert, and always use some softening, mitigating expression, — such as, *s'il m'est permis de le dire; je croirois plutôt; si j'ose m'expliquer*, which soften the manner without giving up or even weakening the thing. People of more age and experience expect and are entitled to that degree of deference.

There is a *bienséance* also with regard to people of the lowest degree; a gentleman observes it with his footman, even with the beggar in the street. He considers them as objects of compassion, not of insult; he speaks to neither *d'un ton brusque*, but corrects the one coolly, and refuses the other with humanity. There is no one occasion in the world in which *le ton brusque* is becoming a gentleman. In short, *les bienséances* are another word for *manners*, and extend to every part of life. They are propriety; the Graces should attend, in order to complete them. The Graces enable us to do, genteelly and pleasingly, what *les bienséances* require to be done at all. The latter are an obligation upon every man; the former are an infinite advantage and ornament to any man. May you unite both!

. . . .

LIII.

THE GRACES.—THE WRITER'S EARLY DEFECTS.— DRESS.

LONDON, *June* 24, O. S. 1751.

MY DEAR FRIEND,—Air, address, manners, and graces are of such infinite advantage to whoever has them, and so peculiarly and essentially necessary for you, that now as the time of our meeting draws near I tremble for fear I should not find you possessed of them; and to tell you the truth, I doubt you are not yet sufficiently convinced of their importance. There is, for instance, your intimate friend Mr. H[ayes], who with great merit, deep knowledge, and a thousand good qualities will never make a figure in the world while he lives. Why? Merely for want of those external and showish accomplishments which he began the world too late to acquire, and which with his studious and philosophical turn, I believe he thinks are not worth his attention. He may very probably make a figure in the republic of letters; but he had ten thousand times better make a figure as a man of the world and of business in the republic of the United Provinces, which, take my word for it, he never will.

As I open myself without the least reserve whenever I think that my doing so can be of any use to you, I will give you a short account of myself when I first came into the world, which was at the age you are of now, so that, by the way, you have got the start of me in that important article by two or three years at least. At nineteen, I left the University of Cambridge, where I was an absolute pedant. When I talked my best, I quoted Horace; when I aimed at being facetious, I quoted Martial; and when I had a mind to be a fine gentleman, I talked Ovid. I was convinced that none but the ancients had common-sense; that the classics contained everything that was either necessary, useful, or ornamental to men; and I was not without thoughts of wearing the *toga virilis* of the Romans instead of the vulgar and illiberal dress of the moderns.[1] With these excellent notions, I went first to the Hague, where, by the help of several letters of recommendation, I was soon introduced into all the best company, and where I very soon discovered that I was totally mistaken in almost every one notion I had entertained. Fortunately, I had a strong desire to please (the mixed result of good-nature and a vanity by no means blameable) and was sensible that I had nothing but the desire. I therefore resolved, if possible, to acquire the means too. I studied attentively and minutely

[1] " Yet there is reason to suspect that this was not the real fact with himself, but only an encouraging example held forth to his son to show him how pedantry may be successfully surmounted." (Lord Mahon.)

the dress, the air, the manner, the address, and the turn of conversation of all those whom I found to be the people in fashion and most generally allowed to please. I imitated them as well as I could; if I heard that one man was reckoned remarkably genteel, I carefully watched his dress, motions, and attitudes, and formed my own upon them. When I heard of another whose conversation was agreeable and engaging, I listened and attended to the turn of it. I addressed myself, though *de très mauvaise grace*, to all the most fashionable fine ladies; confessed, and laughed with them at my own awkwardness and rawness, recommending myself as an object for them to try their skill in forming. By these means, and with a passionate desire of pleasing everybody, I came by degrees to please some; and I can assure you that what little figure I have made in the world has been much more owing to that passionate desire of pleasing universally than to any intrinsic merit or sound knowledge I might ever have been master of. My passion for pleasing was so strong (and I am very glad it was so) that I own to you fairly, I wished to make every woman I saw in love with me and every man I met with admire me. Without this passion for the object, I should never have been so attentive to the means; and I own I cannot conceive how it is possible for any man of good nature and good sense to be without this passion. Does not good nature incline us to please all those we converse with, of whatever rank or station they may be? And does not good sense and common observation show of what infinite use it is to please? Oh! but one may please by the good qualities of the heart and the knowledge of the head, without that fashionable air, address, and manner, which is mere tinsel. I deny it. A man may be esteemed and respected, but I defy him to please without them. Moreover, at your age I would not have contented myself with barely pleasing; I wanted to shine and to distinguish myself in the world as a man of fashion and gallantry, as well as business. And that ambition or vanity, call it what you please, was a right one; it hurt nobody, and made me exert whatever talents I had. It is the spring of a thousand right and good things.

I was talking you over the other day with one very much your friend, and who had often been with you, both at Paris and in Italy. Among the innumerable questions which you may be sure I asked him concerning you, I happened to mention your dress (for, to say the truth, it was the only thing of which I thought him a competent judge), upon which he said that you dressed tolerably well at Paris; but that in Italy you dressed so ill that he used to joke with you upon it, and even to tear your clothes. Now, I must tell you that at your age it is as ridiculous not to be very well dressed as at my age it would be if I were to wear a white feather and red-heeled shoes. Dress is one of various ingredients that contribute to the art of pleasing; it pleases the eyes at least, and more especially of women. Address yourself to the senses, if you would please; dazzle the eyes, soothe and flatter the ears of mankind; engage their hearts, and let their reason do its worst against you. *Suaviter in modo* is the great secret. Whenever you find yourself engaged insensibly in favor of anybody of no superior merit nor distinguished talents, examine and see what it is that has made those impressions upon you, and you will find it to be that *douceur*, that gentleness of manners, that air and address, which I have so often recommended to you; and from thence draw this obvious conclusion, — that what pleases you in them, will please others in you, for we are all made of the same clay, though some of the lumps are a little finer and some a little coarser; but in general the surest way to judge of others is to examine and analyze one's self thoroughly. When we meet I will assist you in that analysis, in which every man wants some assistance against his own self-love. Adieu.

LIV.

ENGLISH AND FRENCH PLAYS COMPARED.

LONDON, *Jan.* 23. O. S. 1752.

MY DEAR FRIEND, — Have you seen the new tragedy of "Varon"[1] and what do you think of it? Let me know, for I am determined to form my taste upon yours. I hear that the situations and incidents are well brought on and the catastrophe

---

[1] Written by the Vicomte de Grave, and at that time the general topic of conversation at Paris.

unexpected and surprising, but the verses bad. I suppose it is the subject of all the conversations at Paris, where both women and men are judges and critics of all such performances. Such conversations that both form and improve the taste and whet the judgment are surely preferable to the conversations of our mixed companies here, which if they happen to rise above bragg and whist infallibly stop short of everything either pleasing or instructive. I take the reason of this to be that (as women generally give the *ton* to the conversation) our English women are not near so well informed and cultivated as the French; besides that they are naturally more serious and silent.

I could wish there were a treaty made between the French and English theatres in which both parties should make considerable concessions. The English ought to give up their notorious violations of all the unities, and all their massacres, racks, dead bodies, and mangled carcasses which they so frequently exhibit upon their stage. The French should engage to have more action and less declamation; and not to cram and crowd things together to almost a degree of impossibility from a too scrupulous adherence to the unities. The English should restrain the licentiousness of their poets and the French enlarge the liberty of theirs: their poets are the greatest slaves in their country, and that is a bold word; ours are the most tumultuous subjects in England, and that is saying a good deal. Under such regulations one might hope to see a play in which one should not be lulled to sleep by the length of a monotonical declamation nor frightened and shocked by the barbarity of the action; the unity of time extended occasionally to three or four days and the unity of place broke into as far as the same street, or sometimes the same town, — both which I will affirm are as probable as four-and-twenty hours and the same room.

More indulgence too, in my mind, should be shown than the French are willing to allow to bright thoughts and to shining images; for though I confess it is not very natural for a hero or a princess to say fine things in all the violence of grief, love, rage, etc., yet I can as well suppose that as I can that they should talk to themselves for half an hour; which they must necessarily do or no tragedy could be carried on, unless they had recourse to a much greater absurdity, — the choruses of the ancients. Tragedy is of a nature that one must see it with a degree of self-deception; we must lend ourselves a little to the delusion; and I am very willing to carry that complaisance a little farther than the French do.

Tragedy must be something bigger than life or it would not effect us. In Nature the most violent passions are silent; in tragedy they must speak, and speak with dignity too. Hence the necessity of their being written in verse, and unfortunately for the French, from the weakness of their language, in rhymes. And for the same reason Cato the Stoic, expiring at Utica, rhymes masculine and feminine at Paris, and fetches his last breath at London in most harmonious and correct blank verse.

It is quite otherwise with comedy, which should be mere common life and not one jot bigger. Every character should speak upon the stage, not only what it would utter in the situation there represented, but in the same manner in which it would express it. For which reason I cannot allow rhymes in comedy, unless they were put into the mouth and came out of the mouth of a mad poet. But it is impossible to deceive one's self enough (nor is it the least necessary in comedy) to suppose a dull rogue of a usurer cheating, or *gros Jean* blundering, in the finest rhymes in the world.

As for operas they are essentially too absurd and extravagant to mention. I look upon them as a magic scene contrived to please the eyes and the ears, at the expense of the understanding; and I consider singing, rhyming, and chiming heroes and princesses and philosophers, as I do the hills, the trees, the birds, and the beasts who amicably joined in one common country-dance to the irresistible turn of Orpheus's lyre. Whenever I go to an opera I leave my sense and reason at the door with my half guinea, and deliver myself up to my eyes and my ears.

. . . .

LV.

UTILITY OF AIMING AT PERFECTION.

LONDON, *Feb.* 20, O. S. 1752.

MY DEAR FRIEND, — In all systems whatsoever, whether of religion, government, morals, etc., perfection is the object always proposed, though possibly unattainable, — hitherto at least certainly unattained. However, those who aim carefully at the mark itself will unquestionably come nearer it than those who from despair, negligence, or indolence leave to chance the work of skill. This maxim holds equally true in common life; those who aim at perfection will come infinitely nearer it than those desponding or indolent spirits who foolishly say to themselves, "Nobody is perfect; perfection is unattainable; to attempt it is chimerical; I shall do as well as others; why then should I give myself trouble to be what I never can, and what according to the common course of things I need not be, — *perfect?*"

I am very sure that I need not point out to you the weakness and the folly of this reasoning, if it deserves the name of reasoning. It would discourage and put a stop to the exertion of any one of our faculties. On the contrary a man of sense and spirit says to himself, "Though the point of perfection may (considering the imperfection of our nature) be unattainable, my care, my endeavors, my attention, shall not be wanting to get as near it as I can. I will approach it every day; possibly I may arrive at it at last; at least — what I am sure is in my own power — I will not be distanced." Many fools (speaking of you) say to me, "What! would you have him perfect?" I answer, Why not? What hurt would it do him or me? "Oh, but that is impossible," say they; I reply I am not sure of that: perfection in the abstract I admit to be unattainable, but what is commonly called perfection in a character I maintain to be attainable, and not only that but in every man's power. " He has," continue they, "a good head, a good heart, a good fund of knowledge, which would increase daily: what would you have more?" Why, I would have everything more that can adorn and complete a character. Will it do his head, his heart, or his knowledge any harm to have the utmost delicacy of manners, the most shining advantages of air and address, the most endearing attentions and the most engaging graces? "But as he is," say they, "he is loved wherever he is known." I am very glad of it, say I; but I would have him be liked before he is known and loved afterwards. I would have him by his first *abord* and address, make people wish to know him, and inclined to love him; he will save a great deal of time by it. "Indeed," reply they, "you are too nice, too exact, and lay too much stress upon things that are of very little consequence." Indeed, rejoin I, you know very little of the nature of mankind if you take those things to be of little consequence; one cannot be too attentive to them; it is they that always engage the heart, of which the understanding is commonly the bubble. And I would much rather that he erred in a point of grammar, of history, of philosophy, etc., than in point of manners and address. "But consider, he is very young: all this will come in time." I hope so; but that time must be when he is young or it will never be at all; the right *pli* must be taken young, or it will never be easy or seem natural. "Come, come," say they (substituting as is frequently done, assertion instead of argument), " depend upon it he will do very well; and you have a great deal of reason to be satisfied with him." I hope and believe he will do well but I would have him do better than well. I am very well pleased with him but I would be more, — I would be proud of him. I would have him have lustre as well as weight. " Did you ever know anybody that re-united all these talents?" Yes, I did; Lord Bolingbroke joined all the politeness, the manners, and the graces of a courtier to the solidity of a statesman and to the learning of a pedant. He was *omnis homo;* and pray what should hinder my boy from being so too, if he has as I think he has all the other qualifications that you allow him? Nothing can hinder him but neglect of or inattention to those objects which his own good sense must tell him are of infinite consequence to him, and which therefore I will not suppose him capable of either neglecting or despising.

This (to tell you the whole truth) is the result of a controversy that passed yesterday between Lady Hervey and myself, upon your subject and almost in the very words. I submit the decision of it to yourself; let your own good sense determine it, and make you act in consequence of that determination. The receipt to make this composition is short and infallible; here I give it you: —

Take variety of the best company wherever you are; be minutely attentive to every word and action; imitate respectively those whom you observe to be distinguished and considered for any one accomplishment; then mix all those several accomplishments together and serve them up yourself to others.

. . . .

LVI.

THE STUDY OF THE WORLD. — COMPANY THE ONLY SCHOOL.

LONDON, *March* 16, O. S. 1752.

MY DEAR FRIEND, — How do you go on with the most useful and most necessary of all studies, — the study of the world? Do you find that you gain knowledge; and does your daily experience at once extend and demonstrate your improvement? You will possibly ask me how you can judge of that yourself. I will tell you a sure way of knowing. Examine yourself and see whether your notions of the world are changed by experience from what they were two years ago in theory; for that alone is one favorable symptom of improvement. At that age (I remember it in myself) every notion that one forms is erroneous; one has seen few models and those none of the best to form one's self upon. One thinks that everything is to be carried by spirit and vigor; that art is meanness, and that versatility and complaisance are the refuge of pusillanimity and weakness. This most mistaken opinion gives an indelicacy, a *brusquerie*, and a roughness to the manners. Fools, who can never be undeceived, retain them as long as they live; reflection with a little experience makes men of sense shake them off soon. When they come to be a little better acquainted with themselves and with their own species, they discover that plain right reason is nine times in ten the fettered and shackled attendant of the triumph of the heart and the passions; and consequently they address themselves nine times in ten to the conqueror, not to the conquered: and conquerors you know must be applied to in the gentlest, the most engaging, and the most insinuating manner. Have you found out that every woman is infallibly to be gained by every sort of flattery, and every man by one sort or other? Have you discovered what variety of little things affect the heart and how surely they collectively gain it? If you have, you have made some progress. I would try a man's knowledge of the world as I would a schoolboy's knowledge of Horace, — not by making him construe *Mæcenas atavis edite regibus*, which he could do in the first form, but by examining him as to the delicacy and *curiosa felicitas* of that poet. A man requires very little knowledge and experience of the world to understand glaring, high-colored, and decided characters; they are but few and they strike at first. But to distinguish the almost imperceptible shades and the nice gradations of virtue and vice, sense and folly, strength and weakness (of which characters are commonly composed), demands some experience, great observation, and minute attention. In the same cases most people do the same things, but with this material difference, upon which the success commonly turns, — a man who has studied the world knows when to time and where to place them; he has analyzed the characters he applies to, and adapted his address and his arguments to them : but a man of what is called plain good sense, who has only reasoned by himself and not acted with mankind, mistimes, misplaces, runs precipitately and bluntly at the mark, and falls upon his nose in the way. In the common manners of social life every man of common-sense has the rudiments, the A B C of civility; he means not to offend and even wishes to please, and if he has any real merit will be received and tolerated in good company. But that is far from being enough; for though he may be received he will never be desired; though he does not offend he will never be loved; but like some little, insignificant, neutral power surrounded by great ones, he will neither be feared nor courted by any, but by turns invaded by all, whenever it is their interest. A most contemptible situation! Whereas a man who has carefully attended to and experienced the various workings of the heart and the artifices of the head, and who by one shade can trace the progression of the whole color; who can at the proper times employ all the several means of persuading the understanding, and engaging the heart, may and will have enemies, but will and must have friends. He may be opposed, but he will be supported too; his talents may excite the jealousy of some, but his engaging arts will make him beloved by many more; he will be considerable; he will be considered. Many different qualifications must conspire to form such a man, and to make him at once respectable and amiable; and the least must be joined to the greatest; the latter would be unavailing without the former, and the former would be futile and frivolous without the latter. Learning is acquired by reading books; but the much more necessary learning, the knowledge of the world, is only to be acquired by reading men and studying all the various editions of them. Many words in every language are generally thought to be synonymous; but those who study the language attentively will find that there is no such thing. They will discover some little difference, some distinction between all those words that are vulgarly called synonymous; one has always more energy, extent, or delicacy than another. It is the same with men; all are in general, and yet no two in particular, exactly alike. Those who have not accurately studied, perpetually mistake them; they do not discern the shades and gradations that distinguish characters seemingly alike. Company, various company, is the only school for this knowledge. You ought to be by this time at least in the third form of that school from whence the rise to the uppermost is easy and quick; but then you must have application and vivacity, and you must not only bear with but even seek restraint in most companies instead of stagnating in one or two only where indolence and love of ease may be indulged.

. . . .

LVII.

HOW HISTORY SHOULD BE WRITTEN.—LOUIS XIV.

LONDON, *April* 13, O. S. 1752.

. . . .

VOLTAIRE sent me from Berlin his history "du Siècle de Louis XIV." It came at a very proper time: Lord Bolingbroke had just taught me how history should be read; Voltaire shows me how it should be written. I am sensible that it will meet with almost as many critics as readers. Voltaire must be criticised: besides, every man's favorite is attacked, for every prejudice is exposed, and our prejudices are our mistresses; reason is at best our wife, very often heard indeed, but seldom minded. It is the history of the human understanding written by a man of parts for the use of men of parts. Weak minds will not like it, even though they do not understand it,—which is commonly the measure of their admiration. Dull ones will want those minute and uninteresting details with which most other histories are encumbered. He tells me all I want to know and nothing more. His reflections are short, just, and produce others in his readers. Free from religious, philosophical, political, and national prejudices beyond any historian I ever met with, he relates all those matters as truly and as impartially as certain regards, which must always be to some degree observed, will allow him: for one sees plainly that he often says much less than he would say if he might. He has made me much better acquainted with the times of Louis XIV. than the innumerable volumes which I had read could do; and has suggested this reflection to me which I have never made before, — his vanity, not his knowledge, made him encourage all and introduce many arts and sciences in his country. He opened in a manner the human understanding in France and brought it to its utmost perfection; his age equalled in all, and greatly exceeded in many things (pardon me, pedants!), the Augustan. This was great and rapid; but still it might be done by the encouragement, the applause and the rewards of a vain, liberal, and magnificent prince. What is much more surprising is, that he stopped the operations of the human mind just where he pleased, and seemed to say, "Thus far shalt thou go, and no farther." For, a bigot to his religion, and jealous of his power, free and rational thoughts upon either never entered into a French head during his reign; and the greatest geniuses that ever any age produced never entertained a doubt of the divine right of kings, or the infallibility of the Church. Poets, orators, and philosophers, ignorant of their natural rights, cherished their chains; and blind active faith triumphed in those great minds over silent and passive reason. The reverse of this seems now to be the case in France: reason opens itself; fancy and invention fade and decline.[1]

. . . .

[1] "Chesterfield," says Lord Carnarvon, "foretold the French Revolution when the cloud was not bigger than a man's hand."

LVIII.

AVOIR DU MONDE EXPLAINED AND RECOMMENDED.

LONDON, *April* 30, O. S. 1752.

MY DEAR FRIEND, — *Avoir du monde* is in my opinion a very just and happy expression for having address, manners, and for knowing how to behave properly in all companies; and it implies very truly that a man who has not those accomplishments is not of the world. Without them the best parts are inefficient, civility is absurd, and freedom offensive. A learned parson rusting in his cell at Oxford or Cambridge will reason admirably well upon the nature of man; will profoundly analyze the head, the heart, the reason, the will, the passions, the senses, the sentiments, and all those subdivisions of we know not what; and yet unfortunately he knows nothing of man, for he has not lived with him, and is ignorant of all the various modes, habits, prejudices, and tastes that always influence and often determine him. He views man as he does colors in Sir Isaac Newton's prism, where only the capital ones are seen; but an experienced dyer knows all their various shades and gradations, together with the result of their several mixtures. Few men are of one plain decided color; most are mixed, shaded, and blended, and vary as much from different situations as changeable silks do from different lights. The man *qui a du monde* knows all this from his own experience and observation: the conceited cloistered philosopher knows nothing of it from his own theory; his practice is absurd and improper, and he acts as awkwardly as a man would dance who had never seen others dance nor learned of a dancing-master, but who had only studied the notes by which dances are now pricked down as well as tunes. Observe and imitate, then, the address, the arts, and the manners of those *qui ont du monde;* see by what methods they first make and afterwards improve impressions in their favor. Those impressions are much oftener owing to little causes than to intrinsic merit, which is less volatile and has not so sudden an effect. Strong minds have undoubtedly an ascendant over weak ones, as Galigai Maréchale d'Ancre very justly observed, when to the disgrace and reproach of those times she was executed [1] for having governed Mary of Medicis by the arts of witchcraft and magic. But then ascendant is to be gained by degrees, and by those arts only which experience and the knowledge of the world teaches; for few are mean enough to be bullied, though most are weak enough to be bubbled. I have often seen people of superior governed by people of much inferior parts, without knowing or even suspecting that they were so governed. This can only happen when those people of inferior parts have more worldly dexterity and experience than those they govern. They see the weak and unguarded part, and apply to it; they take it and all the rest follows. Would you gain either men or women — and every man of sense desires to gain both — *il faut du monde.* You have

[1] On the 8th of July, 1617.

had more opportunities than ever any man had at your age of acquiring *ce monde;* you have been in the best companies of most countries at an age when others have hardly been in any company at all. You are master of all those languages which John Trott seldom speaks at all, and never well; consequently you need be a stranger nowhere. This is the way, and the only way, of having *du monde;* but if you have it not, and have still any coarse rusticity about you, may not one apply to you the *rusticus expectat* of Horace?

This knowledge of the world teaches us more particularly two things, both which are of infinite consequence, and to neither of which nature inclines us; I mean, the command of our temper and of our countenance. A man who has no *monde* is inflamed with anger or annihilated with shame at every disagreeable incident; the one makes him act and talk like a madman, the other makes him look like a fool. But a man who has *du monde* seems not to understand what he cannot or ought not to resent. If he makes a slip himself, he recovers it by his coolness, instead of plunging deeper by his confusion, like a stumbling horse. He is firm, but gentle; and practises that most excellent maxim, *suaviter in modo, fortiter in re.* The other is the *volto sciolto e pensieri stretti.*[1] People unused to the world have babbling countenances, and are unskilful enough to show what they have sense enough not to tell. In the course of the world, a man must very often put on an easy, frank counte-

[1] An open countenance and a reserved mind.

nance upon very disagreeable occasions; he must seem pleased when he is very much otherwise; he must be able to accost and receive with smiles those whom he would much rather meet with swords. In Courts he must not turn himself inside out. All this may, nay, must be done, without falsehood and treachery; for it must go no further than politeness and manners, and must stop short of assurances and professions of simulated friendship. Good manners to those one does not love, are no more a breach of truth than "your humble servant" at the bottom of a challenge is; they are universally agreed upon and understood to be things of course. They are necessary guards of the decency and peace of society; they must only act defensively, and then not with arms poisoned with perfidy. Truth, but not the whole truth, must be the invariable principle of every man who has either religion, honor, or prudence. Those who violate it may be cunning, but they are not able. Lies and perfidy are the refuge of fools and cowards. Adieu!

LIX.

ON MILITARY MEN.—SMALL CHANGE.

LONDON, *Sept.* 19, 1752.

. . . .

YOUR attending the parades has also another good effect,—which is that it brings you of course acquainted with the officers, who, when of a certain rank and service, are generally very polite, well bred people, *et du bon ton*. They have commonly seen a great deal of the world and of Courts, — and nothing else can form a gentleman, let people say what they will of sense and learning, with both which a man may contrive to be a very disagreeable companion. I dare say there are very few captains of foot who are not much better company than ever Descartes or Sir Isaac Newton were. I honor and respect such superior geniuses; but I desire to converse with people of this world, who bring into company their share at least of cheerfulness, good breeding, and knowledge of mankind. In common life, one much oftener wants small money and silver than gold. Give me a man who has ready cash about him for present expenses, — sixpences, shillings, half-crowns, and crowns, which circulate easily; but a man who has only an ingot of gold about him is much above common purposes, and his riches are not handy nor convenient. Have as much gold as you please in one pocket, but take care always to keep change in the other; for you will much oftener have occasion for a shilling than for a guinea.

. . . .

LX.

ADAPTATION OF MANNERS TO PERSONS, PLACES, AND TIMES.

LONDON, *Sept.* 22, 1752.

. . . .

THE reception which you have met with at Hanover I look upon as an omen of your being well received everywhere else; for, to tell you the truth, it was the place that I distrusted the most in that particular. But there is a certain conduct, there are *certaines manières* that will and must get the better of all difficulties of that kind; it is to acquire them that you still continue abroad, and go from Court to Court; they are personal, local, and temporal; they are modes which vary and owe their existence to accidents, whim, and humor. All the sense and reason in the world would never point them out; nothing but experience, observation, and what is called knowledge of the world, can possibly teach them. For example, it is respectful to bow to the King of England; it is disrespectful to bow to the King of France; it is the rule to courtesy to the Emperor; and the prostration of the whole body is required by eastern monarchs. These are established ceremonies, and must be complied with; but why they were established, I defy sense and reason to tell us. It is the same among all ranks, where certain customs are received and must necessarily be complied with, though by no means the result of sense and reason. As for instance, the very absurd though almost universal custom of drinking people's healths. Can there be anything in the world less relative to any other man's health than my drinking a glass of wine? Common sense certainly never pointed it out: but yet common sense tells me I must conform to it. Good sense bids one be civil and endeavor to please, though nothing but experience and observation can teach one the means, properly adapted to time, place, and persons. This knowledge is the true object of a gentleman's travelling, if he travels as he ought to do. By frequenting good company in every country, he himself becomes of every country; he is no longer an Englishman, a Frenchman, or an Italian, but he is a European; he adopts, respectively, the best manners of every country, and is a Frenchman at Paris, an Italian at Rome, an Englishman at London.

This advantage, I must confess, very seldom accrues to my countrymen from their travelling, as they have neither the desire nor the means of getting into good company abroad: for, in the first place, they are confoundedly bashful, and in the next place, they either speak no foreign language at all, or, if they do, it is barbarously. You possess all the advantages that they want; you know the languages in perfection, and have constantly kept the best company in the places where you have been; so that you ought to be a European. Your canvas is solid and strong, your outlines are good; but remember that you still want the beautiful coloring of Titian and the delicate graceful touches of Guido. Now is your time to get them. There is in all good company a fashionable air, countenance, manner, and phraseology, which can only be acquired by being in good company, and very attentive to all that passes there. When you dine or sup at any well-bred man's house, observe carefully how he does the honors of his table to the different guests. Attend to the compliments of congratulation or condolence that you hear a well-bred man make to his superiors, to his equals, and to his inferiors; watch even his countenance and his tone of voice, for they all conspire in the main point of pleasing. There is a certain distinguishing diction of a man of fashion; he will not content himself with saying, like John Trott, to a new married man, "Sir, I wish you much joy," or to a man who lost his son, "Sir, I am sorry for your loss," and both with a countenance equally unmoved; but he will say in effect the same thing, in a more elegant and less trivial manner, and with a countenance adapted to the occasion. He will advance with warmth, vivacity, and a cheerful countenance to the new married man, and embracing him, perhaps say to him, "If you do justice to my attachment to you, you will judge of the joy that I feel upon this occasion better than I can express it," etc. To the other in affliction, he will advance slowly, with a grave composure of countenance, in a more deliberate manner, and with a lower voice, perhaps say, "I hope you do me the justice to be convinced that I feel whatever you feel, and shall ever be affected where you are concerned."

Your *abord*, I must tell you was too cold and

uniform; I hope it is now mended. It should be respectfully open and cheerful with your superiors, warm and animated with your equals, hearty and free with your inferiors. There is a fashionable kind of *small talk*, which you should get, which, trifling as it is, is of use in mixed companies and at table, especially in your foreign department, where it keeps off certain serious subjects that might create disputes, or at least coldness for a time. Upon such occasions it is not amiss to know how to *parler cuisine*, and to be able to dissert upon the growth and flavor of wines. These, it is true, are very little things; but they are little things that occur very often, and therefore should be said *avec gentillesse et grace*. I am sure they must fall often in your way; pray take care to catch them. There is a certain language of conversation, a fashionable diction, of which every gentleman ought to be perfectly master, in whatever language he speaks. The French attend to it carefully, and with great reason; and their language, which is a language of phrases, helps them out exceedingly. That delicacy of diction is characteristical of a man of fashion and good company.

I could write folios upon this subject and not exhaust it; but I think and hope that to you I need not. You have heard and seen enough to be convinced of the truth and importance of what I have been so long inculcating into you upon these points How happy am I, and how happy are you, my dear child, that these Titian tints and Guido graces are all that you want to complete my hopes and your own character! But then, on the other hand, what a drawback would it be to that happiness, if you should never acquire them! I remember, when I was of your age, though I had not had near so good an education as you have or seen a quarter so much of the world, I observed those masterly touches and irresistible graces in others, and saw the necessity of acquiring them myself; but then an awkward *mauvaise honte*, of which I had brought a great deal with me from Cambridge, made me ashamed to attempt it, especially if any of my countrymen and particular acquaintance were by. This was extremely absurd in me; for, without attempting, I could never succeed. But at last, insensibly, by frequenting a great deal of good company, and imitating those whom I saw that everybody liked, I formed myself, *tant bien que mal*. For God's sake, let this last fine varnish, so necessary to give lustre to the whole piece, be the sole and single object now of your utmost attention. Berlin may contribute a great deal to it if you please; there are all the ingredients that compose it.

· · · · · · · ·

LXI.

VOLTAIRE, HOMER, VIRGIL, MILTON, AND TASSO. — CHARLES XII. OF SWEDEN NOT A HERO.

BATH, *October* 4, 1752.

MY DEAR FRIEND, — I consider you now as at the court of Augustus,[1] where, if ever the desire of

[1] The court of Frederick II. of Prussia.

pleasing animated you, it must make you exert all the means of doing it. You will see there, full as well, I dare say, as Horace did at Rome, how States are defended by arms, adorned by manners, and improved by laws. Nay, you have an Horace there, as well as an Augustus; I need not name Voltaire, *qui nil molitur inepte,* as Horace himself said of another poet. I have lately read over all his works that are published, though I had read them more than once before. I was induced to this by his " Siècle de Louis XIV.," which I have yet read but four times. In reading over all his works, with more attention I suppose than before, my former admiration of him is, I own, turned into astonishment. There is no one kind of writing in which he has not excelled. You are so severe a classic that I question whether you will allow me to call his "Henriade " an epic poem, for want of the proper number of gods, devils, witches, and other absurdities requisite for the machinery; which machinery is, it seems, necessary to constitute the Epopée. But whether you do or not, I will declare (though possibly to my own shame) that I never read any epic poem with near so much pleasure. I am grown old, and have possibly lost a great deal of that fire which formerly made me love fire in others at any rate, and however attended with smoke ; but now I must have all sense, and cannot for the sake of five righteous lines forgive a thousand absurd ones.

In this disposition of mind, judge whether I can read all Homer through *tout de suite.* I admire his beauties, but to tell you the truth, when he slumbers

I sleep. Virgil, I confess, is all sense, and therefore I like him better than his model; but he is often languid, especially in his five or six last books, during which I am obliged to take a good deal of snuff. Besides, I profess myself an ally of Turnus's against the pious Æneas, who like many *soi disant* pious people, does the most flagrant injustice and violence in order to execute what they impudently call the will of Heaven. But what will you say when I tell you truly that I cannot possibly read our countryman Milton through? I acknowledge him to have some most sublime passages, some prodigious flashes of light; but then you must acknowledge that light is often followed by *darkness visible*, to use his own expression. Besides, not having the honor to be acquainted with any of the parties in his poem, except the man and the woman, the characters and speeches of a dozen or two of angels and of as many devils are as much above my reach as my entertainment. Keep this secret for me; for if it should be known, I should be abused by every tasteless pedant and every solid divine in England.

Whatever I have said to the disadvantage of these three poems holds much stronger against Tasso's "Gierusalemme:" it is true he has very fine and glaring rays of poetry; but then they are only meteors, they dazzle, then disappear, and are succeeded by false thoughts, poor *concetti*, and absurd impossibilities. Witness the Fish and the Parrot; extravagancies unworthy of an heroic poem, and would much better have become Ariosto, who professes *le coglionerie*.

I have never read the Lusiad of Camoens, except in a prose translation, consequently I have never read it at all, so shall say nothing of it; but the "Henriade" is all sense from the beginning to the end, often adorned by the justest and liveliest reflections, the most beautiful descriptions, the noblest images, and the sublimest sentiments, — not to mention the harmony of the verse, in which Voltaire undoubtedly exceeds all the French poets. Should you insist upon an exception in favor of Racine, I must insist on my part that he at least equals him. What hero ever interested more than Henry the Fourth, who according to the rules of epic poetry, carries on one great and long action, and succeeds in it at last? What descriptions ever excited more horror than those, first of the massacre, and then of the famine at Paris? Was love ever painted with more truth and *morbidezza* than in the ninth book? Not better in my mind, even in the fourth of Virgil. Upon the whole, with all your classical rigor, if you will but suppose *St. Louis* a god, a devil, or a witch, and that he appears in person and not in a dream, the " Henriade " will be an epic poem, according to the strictest statute laws of the Epopée; but in my court of equity it is one as it is.

I could expatiate as much upon all his different works but that I should exceed the bounds of a letter, and run into a dissertation. How delightful is his history of that northern brute, the King of Sweden![1] — for I cannot call him a man; and I should

[1] Charles XII. Voltaire's life of that king first appeared in 1731.

be sorry to have him pass for a hero, out of regard to those true heroes, such as Julius Caesar, Titus, Trajan, and the present King of Prussia, who cultivated and encouraged arts and sciences; whose animal courage was accompanied by the tender and social sentiments of humanity; and who had more pleasure in improving than in destroying their fellow-creatures. What can be more touching or more interesting, what more nobly thought or more happily expressed than all his dramatic pieces? What can be more clear and rational than all his philosophical letters; and what ever was so graceful and gentle as all his little poetical trifles? You are fortunately *à portée* of verifying by your knowledge of the man all that I have said of his works.

. . . .

LXII.

A WORTHY, TIRESOME MAN. — MANNERS ADD LUSTRE TO LEARNING.

LONDON, *May* 27, O. S. 1753.

MY DEAR FRIEND, — I have this day been tired, jaded, nay, tormented, by the company of a most worthy, sensible, and learned man, a near relation of mine, who dined and passed the evening with me. This seems a paradox but is a plain truth; he has no knowledge of the world, no manners, no address. Far from talking without book, as is commonly said of people who talk sillily, he only talks by book, — which in general conversation is ten times worse. He has formed in his own closet from books certain systems of everything, argues tenaciously upon those principles, and is both surprised and angry at whatever deviates from them. His theories are good but unfortunately are all impracticable. Why? because he has only read and not conversed. He is acquainted with books and an absolute stranger to men. Laboring with his matter he is delivered of it with pangs; he hesitates, stops in his utterance, and always expresses himself inelegantly. His actions are all ungraceful; so that with all his merit and knowledge, I would rather converse six hours with the most frivolous tittle-tattle woman who knew something of the world than with him. The preposterous notions of a systematical man who does not know the world tire the patience of a man who does. It would be endless to correct his mistakes, nor would he take it kindly, for he has considered everything deliberately and is very sure that he is in the right. Impropriety is a characteristic, and a never-failing one, of these people. Regardless, because ignorant, of customs and manners, they violate them every moment. They often shock though they never mean to offend, never attending either to the general character or the particular distinguishing circumstances of the people to whom or before whom they talk; whereas the knowledge of the world teaches one that the very same things which are exceedingly right and proper in one company, time, and place are exceedingly absurd in others. In short, a man who has great knowledge from experience and observation of the character, customs, and manners of mankind is a being as different from and as superior to a man of mere book and systematical knowledge as a well-managed horse is to an ass. Study therefore, cultivate, and frequent men and women, — not only in their outward, and consequently guarded, but in their interior, domestic, and consequently less disguised characters and manners. Take your notions of things as by observation and experience you find they really are, and not as you read that they are or should be, for they never are quite what they should be. For this purpose do not content yourself with general and common acquaintance, but wherever you can, establish yourself with a kind of domestic familiarity in good houses. For instance, go again to Orli for two or three days and so at two or three *reprises*. Go and stay two or three days at a time at Versailles and improve and extend the acquaintance you have there. Be at home at St. Cloud, and whenever any private person of fashion invites you to pass a few days at his country-house accept of the invitation. This will necessarily give you a versatility of mind and a facility to adopt various manners and customs; for everybody desires to please those in whose house they are, and people are only to be pleased in their own way. Nothing is more engaging than a cheerful and easy conformity to people's particular manners, habits, and even weaknesses; nothing (to use a vulgar expression) should come amiss to a young fellow. He should be for good purposes what Alcibiades was commonly for bad ones, — a Proteus assuming with ease and wearing with cheerfulness any shape. Heat, cold, luxury, abstinence, gravity, gayety, ceremony, easiness, learning, trifling, business, and pleasure are modes which he should be able to take, lay aside, or change occasionally with as much ease as he would take or lay aside his hat. All this is only to be acquired by use and knowledge of the world, by keeping a great deal of company, analyzing every character, and insinuating yourself into the familiarity of various acquaintance. A right, a generous ambition to make a figure in the world, necessarily gives the desire of pleasing; the desire of pleasing points out to a great degree the means of doing it; and the art of pleasing is in truth the art of rising, of distinguishing one's self, of making a figure and a fortune in the world. But without pleasing, without the Graces, as I have told you a thousand times, *ogni fatica è vana*. You are now but nineteen, an age at which most of your countrymen are illiberally getting drunk in port at the University. You have greatly got the start of them in learning, and if you can equally get the start of them in the knowledge and manners of the world, you may be very sure of outrunning them in Court and Parliament, as you set out so much earlier than they. They generally begin but to see the world at one and twenty; you will by that age have seen all Europe. They set out upon their travels unlicked cubs, and in their travels they only lick one another, for they seldom go into any other company. They know nothing but the English world, and the worst part of that too, and generally very little of any but the English language, and they come home at three or four-and-twenty refined and polished (as is said in one of Congreve's plays) like Dutch skippers from a whale-fishing. The care which has been taken of you, and to do you justice the care that you have taken of yourself, has left you at the age of nineteen only nothing to acquire but the knowledge of the world, manners, address, and those exterior accomplishments. But they are great and necessary acquisitions to those who have sense enough to know their true value, and your getting them before you are one and twenty and before you enter upon the active and shining scene of life will give you such an advantage over your contemporaries that they cannot overtake you; they must be distanced. You may probably be placed about a young prince who will probably be a young king. There all the various arts of pleasing, the engaging address, the versatility of manners, the *brillant*, the Graces, will outweigh and yet outrun all solid knowledge and unpolished merit. Oil yourself therefore, and be both supple and shining for that race if you would be first, or early at the goal. Ladies will most probably too have something to say there, and those who are best with them will probably be best *somewhere else*. Labor this great point, my dear child, indefatigably; attend to the very smallest parts, the minutest graces, the most trifling circumstances that can possibly concur in forming the shining character of a complete gentleman, *un galant homme, un homme de cour*, a man of business and pleasure, *estimé des hommes, recherché des femmes, aimé de tout le monde.*

In this view, observe the shining part of every man of fashion who is liked and esteemed; attend to and imitate that particular accomplishment for which you hear him chiefly celebrated and distinguished; then collect those various parts and make yourself a mosaic of the whole. No one body possesses everything, and almost everybody possesses some one thing worthy of imitation; only choose your models well, and in order to do so, choose by your ear more than by your eye. The best model is always that which is most universally allowed to be the best, though in strictness it may possibly not be so. We must take most things as they are; we cannot make them what we would nor often what they should be, and where moral duties are not concerned, it is more prudent to follow than to attempt to lead. Adieu.

LETTERS OF LORD CHESTERFIELD TO HIS GODSON.

LETTERS OF LORD CHESTERFIELD TO HIS GODSON.

I.

DIVERSION ORDERED, STUDY REQUESTED, IGNORANCE DESPISED.

LONDON, *Nov.* 3, 1761.

MAY it please your honor,[1] see how punctual I am. I received your letter but yesterday, and I do myself the honor of answering it to-day. You tell me that when you are at Monsieur Robert's, you will obey my orders, but that is a very unlimited engagement, for how do you know what orders I shall give you? As for example, suppose I should order you to play and divert yourself heartily, would you do it? And yet that will be one of my orders. It is true I shall desire you at your leisure hours to mind your reading, your writing, and your French; but that will be only a request which you may comply with or not as you please; for no man who does not desire to know and to be esteemed in the world should be forced to it, for it is punishment enough to be a blockhead and to be despised in all companies.

[1] The boy was in his seventh year at the date of this letter.

I fancy you have a good memory; and from time to time, young as it is, I shall put it to the trial; for whatever you get by heart at this age you will remember as long as you live, and therefore I send you these fine verses of Mr. Dryden, and give you a whole month to get them by heart.

> " When I consider life, 't is all a cheat;
> Yet fool'd with hope, men favor the deceit,
> Trust on, and think to-morrow will repay.
> To-morrow's falser than the former day;
> Lies worse, and when it bids us most be blest
> With some new hope, cuts off what we possess.
> Fond cozenage this; who 'd live past years again?
> Yet all hope pleasure from what still remain;
> And from the dregs of life think to receive
> What the first sprightly runnings could not give.
> I 'm tired of seeking for this chymick gold,
> Which fools us young, and beggars us when old.

II.

DUTY TO GOD, AND DUTY TO MAN.

Aug. 2 [1762].

DEAR PHIL, — Though I generally write to you upon those subjects which you are now chiefly employed in, such as history, geography, and French, yet I must from time to time remind you of two much more important duties which I hope you will never forget nor neglect. I mean your duty to God and your duty to man. God has been so good as to write in all our hearts the duty that he expects from us, which is adoration and thanksgiving, and doing all the good we can to our fellow creatures. Our conscience, if we will but consult and attend to it, never fails to remind us of those duties. I dare say that you feel an inward pleasure when you have learned your book well and have been a good boy, as on the other hand I am sure you feel an inward uneasiness when you have not done so. This is called "conscience," which I hope you will always consult and follow. You owe all the advantages you enjoy to God, who can and who probably will take them away whenever you are ungrateful to him, for he has justice as well as mercy. Get by heart the four following and excellent lines of Voltaire, and retain them in your mind as long as you live : —

> "Dieu nous donna les biens, il veut qu'on en jouisse ;
> Mais n'oubliés jamais leur cause et leur Auteur ;
> Et quand vous goûtez sa Divine faveur,
> O Mortels, gardez vous d'oublier sa justice."

Your duty to man is very short and clear, — it is only to do to him whatever you would be willing that he should do to you. And remember in all the business of your life to ask your conscience this question: "Should I be willing that this should be done to me?" If your conscience, which will always tell you truth, answers NO, do not do that thing. Observe these rules, and you will be happy in this world and still happier in the next. Bon soir, mon petit bout d'homme.

CHESTERFIELD.

III.

ROUGH MANNERS: JOHN TROTT, THE TWO-LEGGED BEAR.

BLACK-HEATH, *Aug.* 18 [1762].

DEAR PHIL, — I cannot enough inculcate into you the absolute necessity and infinite advantages of pleasing; that is, *d'être aimable;* and it is so easy to be so that I am surprised at the folly or stupidity of those who neglect it. The first great step towards pleasing is to desire to please, and whoever really desires it will please to a certain degree. La douceur et la politesse dans l'air et dans les manières plairont toujours. I am very sorry to tell you that you have not *l'air de la politesse;* for you have got an odious trick of not looking people in the face who speak to you, or whom you speak to. This is a most shocking trick, and implies guilt, fear, or inattention; and you must absolutely be cured of it or nobody will love you. You know what stress both your father and I lay upon it, and we shall neither of us love you till you are broke of it. I am sure you would not be called John Trott, and both I and others will call you so if you are not more attentive and polite. I believe you do not know who this same John Trott is. He is a character in a play of a brutal, bearish Englishman; for there are English two-legged bears, and but too many of them. He is rude, inattentive, and rough, seldom bows to people, and never looks them in the face. After this description of him, tell me which would you choose to be called, John Trott or a well-bred gentleman. C'est a dire voudriez-vous étre aimable, ou brutal. Il n'y a point de milieu; il faut opter et étre l'un ou l'autre. I know which you will choose, — I am sure you will desire and endeavor to be *aimable*.

. . . .

IV.

THE WELL-BRED GENTLEMAN.

Monday Morning [1762].

DEAR PHIL, — You say that you will not be John Trott, and you are in the right of it, for I should be very sorry to call you John Trott, and should not love you half so well as I do, if you deserved that name. The lowest and the poorest people in the world expect good breeding from a gentleman, and they have a right to it, for they are by nature your equals, and are no otherwise your inferiors than by their education and their fortune. Therefore whenever you speak to people who are no otherwise your inferiors than by these circumstances, you must remember to look them in the face, and to speak to them with great humanity and *douceur*, or else they will think you proud and hate you. I am sure you would rather be loved than either hated or laughed at, and yet I can assure [you] that you will be either hated or laughed at if you do not make yourself *aimable*. You will ask me perhaps what you must do to be *aimable*. Do but resolve to be so and the business is almost done. *Ayez seulement de la politesse, de la douceur, et des attentions, et je vous reponds que vous serez aimé, et d'autant plus, que les Anglois ne sont pas généralement aimables.* Among attentions, one of the most material ones is to look people in the face when they speak to you or when you speak to them, and this I insist upon your doing, or upon my word I shall be very angry. Another thing I charge you always to do; which is, when you come into a room, or go out of it, to make a bow to the company. All this I dare say you will do, because I am sure that you would rather be called a well-bred gentleman than John Trott. I therefore send you this pocket-book, and will one day this week send for you to dine with me at Black-heath, before the days grow too short. *Adieu; soyez honnête homme.*

CHESTERFIELD.

V.

SOME RULES FOR THE BEHAVIOR OF A WELL-BRED GENTLEMAN.

[1762.]

DEAR PHIL, — As I know that you desire to be a well-bred gentleman and not a two-legged bear, and to be beloved instead of being hated or laughed at, I send you some general rules for your behavior, which will make you not only be loved but admired. You must have great attention to everything that passes where you are, in order to do what will be most agreeable to the company.

Whoever you speak to, or whoever speaks to you, you must be sure to look them full in the face. For it is not only ill bred, but brutal, either to look upon the ground or to have your eyes wandering about the room, when people are speaking to you or you are speaking to them. When people speak to you, though they do not directly ask you a question you must give them an answer, and not let them think that you are deaf or that you do not care what they say. For example, if a person says to you "This [is] a very hot day," you must say, "yes" or "No, sir."

You must call every gentleman "sir" or "my lord," and every woman "madam." . . .

When you are at dinner you must sit upright in your chair, and not loll. And when anybody offers to help you to anything, if you will have it you must say, "Yes, if you will be so good," or, "I am ashamed to give you so much trouble." If you will not have it you must say, "No, thank you," or, "I am very much obliged to you." You must drink first to the mistress of the house and next to the master of it.

When you first come into a room you must not fail to make a bow to the company, and also when you go out of it.

You must never look sullen or pouting, but have a cheerful, easy countenance.

Remember that there is no one thing so necessary for a gentleman as to be perfectly civil and well bred. Nobody was ever loved that was not well bred; and to tell you the truth, neither your papa nor I shall love you if you are not well bred, and I am sure you desire that we should both love you, as we do now, because you are a very good boy. And so God bless you.

VI.

THE ART OF PLEASING: SACRIFICE TO THE GRACES.

À BATH, 12 *Decem.*, 1763.

Vous dites que vous souhaittez de briller dans le monde, et vous avez raison, car on n'y est point placé simplement pour boire et pour manger. Vous qui etes né avec du bon sens naturel, il vous est aisé de vous distinguer dans le monde, si vous le voulez veritablement, mais il ne faut pas perdre du temps, il faut commencer a votre age, ou bien vous n'y parviendrez jamais. Il n'y a que deux choses a faire pour cela, et qui dependent absolument de vous, qui sont d'être tres poli et tres savant. Si vous êtes savant, mais sans politesse et sans manieres, vous pourrez peut-être, être estimé, mais jamais être aimé. De l'autre coté si vous êtes poli, mais ignorant, on ne vous haïra pas a la verité, mais on vous meprisera, et on se mocquera de vous. Il faut donc necessairement vous rendre en même temps aimable et estimable, si vous voulez briller, — aimable par vos manieres douces et polies, par vos attentions, par un air prevenant, par les Graces; et estimable par votre savoir. Le grand art, et le plus necessaire de tous, c'est *l'art de plaire*. Vouloir tout de bon plaire, est bien la moitié du chemin pour y parvenir, le reste depend de l'observation et de l'usage du monde, dont je vous parlerai fort souvent dans la suite ; mais en attendant, cherchez a plaire autant que vous le pourrez, et faites vos petites remarques de tout ce qui vous plait ou vous deplait dans les autres, et comptez qu'a peu pres les mêmes choses en vous plairont ou deplairont aux autres. Pour les moyens de plaire, ils sont infinis, mais je vous les developperai peu a peu selon que votre âge le permettra, a present je me contenterai, si vous prenez une forte resolution de plaire autant que vous le pourrez. *Sacrifiez toujours aux Graces.*

. . . .

VII.

FLAT CONTRADICTION A PROOF OF ILL BREEDING.— AN EPIGRAM.—SIMILES AND METAPHORS.

July 13, 1764.

I shall sometimes correspond with my giddy little boy in English,[1] that he may not be a stranger to his own language; for though it is very useful and becoming to a gentleman to speak several languages well, it is most absolutely necessary for him to speak his own native language correctly and elegantly, not to be laughed at in every company. It is a terrible thing to be ridiculous, and little things will make a man so. For instance, not writing nor spelling well makes any man ridiculous, but above all things being ill bred makes a man not only ridiculous but hated. I am sure you know that it is

[1] Many of Lord Chesterfield's earlier letters to his godson were written in French.

your most important moral duty to do to others what you would have them do to you; and would you have them civil to you and endeavor to please you? To be sure you would; consequently it is your duty as well as your interest to be civil to, and to endeavor to please, them. There is no greater mark of ill breeding than contradicting people bluntly, and saying, "No," or "It is not so;" and I will give you warning that if you say so, you will be called Phil Trott, of Mansfield, and perhaps you would never get off of that name as long as you live, for ridicule sticks a great while. When well-bred people contradict anybody, they say, instead of "No," "I ask pardon, but I take it to be otherwise," or "It seems to me to be the contrary;" but a flat "No" is as much the same as saying "You lie;" for which if you were a man you would be knocked down, and perhaps run through the body. To refresh your English, I send you here a pretty little gallant epigram, written upon a lady's fan by the late Bishop of Rochester, Dr. Atterbury.

> " Flavia the least and slightest toy
> Can with resistless art employ.
> This fan in other hands would prove
> An engine of small force in love;
> But she with matchless air and mien,
> Not to be told nor safely seen,
> Directs its wanton motions so,
> It wounds us more than Cupid's bow,
> Gives coolness to the matchless dame,
> To every other breast a flame.

This epigram you see turns upon the flame of love, which is a common metaphor used by lovers, and the coolness that fanning gives. But you will naturally ask me what is a metaphor, and I will tell you that it is a short simile, but then what is a simile? A simile is a comparison, as for example, if you should say that Charles the Twelfth of Sweden was as brave as a lion, that would be a simile, because you compare him to a lion; but if you said that Charles the Twelfth was a lion, that would be a metaphor, because you do not say that he was like a lion, but that he was a lion. Do you understand this? Good-night, my little boy; be attentive to your book, well bred in company, and alive at your play. Be *totus in illis*.

VIII.

DO UNTO OTHERS AS YOU WOULD THEY SHOULD DO UNTO YOU.

BATH, *Nov.* 7, 1765.

MY DEAR LITTLE BOY, — The desire of being pleased is universal; the desire of pleasing should be so too, — it is included in that great and fundamental principle of morality, of doing to others what one wishes that they should do to us. There are indeed some moral duties of a much higher but none of a more amiable nature, and I do not hesitate to place it at the head of what Cicero calls the "leniores virtutes." The benevolent and feeling heart performs this duty with pleasure, and in a manner that gives it at the same time; but the great, the rich, and the powerful too often bestow their favors upon their inferiors in a manner that they bestow their scraps upon their dogs, — so as neither to oblige man nor dog. It is no wonder if favors, benefits, and even charities, thus ungraciously bestowed, should be as coldly and faintly acknowledged. Gratitude is a burden upon our imperfect nature, and we are but too willing to ease ourselves of it, or at least to lighten it as much as we can. The manner therefore of conferring favors or benefits is as to pleasing almost as important as the matter itself. Take care, then, never to throw away the obligations which you may perhaps have it in your power to lay upon others, by an air of insolent protection, or by a cold, comfortless, and perfunctory manner, which stifles them in their birth. Humanity inclines, religion requires, and our moral duty obliges us to relieve as far as we are able the distresses and miseries of our fellow creatures; but this is not all, for a true, heartfelt benevolence and tenderness will prompt us to contribute what we can to their ease, their amusement, and their pleasure as far as innocently we may. Let us then not only scatter benefits but even strew flowers for our fellow travellers in the rugged ways of this wretched world. There are some, and but too many in this country more particularly, who without the least visible taint of ill-nature or malevolence seem to be totally indifferent, and do not show the least desire to please, as on the other hand they never designedly offend. Whether this proceeds from a lazy, negligent, and listless disposition, from a gloomy and melancholic nature, from ill health and low spirits, or from a secret and sullen pride arising from the consciousness of their boasted liberty and independency, is hard to determine, considering the various movements of the human heart, and the wonderful errors of the human mind; but be the cause what it will, that neutrality which is the effect of it makes these people, as neutralities always do, despicable, and mere blanks in society. They would surely be roused from this indifference, if they would seriously consider the *infinite utility of pleasing*, which I shall do in my next.

IX.

ON SELF-COMMAND.

BATH, *Dec.* 12, 1765.

MY DEAR LITTLE BOY, — If you have not command enough over yourself to conquer your humor, as I hope you will and as I am sure every rational creature may have, never go into company while the fit of ill humor is upon you. Instead of companies diverting you in those moments, you will displease and probably shock them, and you will part worse friends than you met. But whenever you find in yourself a disposition to sullenness, contradiction, or testiness, it will be in vain to seek for a cure abroad; stay at home, let your humor ferment, and work itself off. Cheerfulness and good humor are of all qualifications the most amiable in company, for though they do not necessarily imply good-nature and good breeding, they act them at least very well, and that is all that is required in mixed company. I have indeed known some very ill-natured people who are very good-humored in company, but I never knew anybody generally ill-humored in company who was not essentially ill-natured. When there is no malevolence in the heart, there is always a cheerfulness and ease in the countenance and the manners. By good humor and cheerfulness I am far from meaning noisy mirth and loud peals of laughter, which are the distinguishing characteristics of the vulgar and the ill bred, whose mirth is a kind of a storm. Observe it, the vulgar often laugh but never smile, whereas well-bred people often smile and seldom or never laugh. A witty thing never excited laughter; it pleases only the mind and never distorts the countenance. A glaring absurdity, a blunder, a silly accident, and those things that are generally called comical may excite a momentary laugh, though never a loud nor a long one among well-bred people. Sudden passion is called a short-lived madness; it is a madness indeed, but the fits of it generally return so often in choleric people that it may well be called a continual madness. Should you happen to be of this unfortunate disposition, which God forbid, make it your constant study to subdue or at least to check it. When you find your choler rising, resolve neither to speak to nor answer the person who excites it, but stay till you find it subsiding and then speak deliberately. I have known many people who by the rapidity of their speech have run away with themselves into a passion. I will mention to

you a trifling and perhaps you will think a ridiculous
receipt toward checking the excess of passion, of
which I think that I have experienced the utility
myself. Do everything in Menuet time; speak,
think, and move always in that measure, equally
free from the dulness of slow or the hurry and
huddle of quick time. This movement moreover
will allow you some moments to think forwards, and
the Graces to accompany what you say or do, for
they are never represented as either running or
dozing. Observe a man in a passion; see his eyes
glaring, his face inflamed, his limbs trembling, and
his tongue stammering and faulting with rage, and
then ask yourself calmly whether you would upon
any account be that human wild beast. Such creatures are hated and dreaded in all companies where
they are let loose, as people do not choose to be
exposed to the disagreeable necessity of either
knocking down these brutes or being knocked down
by them. Do on the contrary endeavor to be cool
and steady upon all occasions. The advantages of
such a steady calmness are innumerable and would
be too tedious to relate. It may be acquired by
care and reflection. If it could not, that reason
which distinguishes men from brutes would be
given us to very little purpose. As a proof of this
I never saw and scarcely ever heard of a Quaker
in a passion. In truth there is in that sect a decorum, a decency, and an amiable simplicity that
I know in no other. Having mentioned the Graces
in this letter, I cannot end it without recommending
to you most earnestly the advice of the wisest of the

ancients, — to sacrifice to them devoutly and daily. When they are propitious they adorn everything and engage everybody. But are they to be acquired? Yes, to a certain degree they are, by attention, observation, and assiduous worship. Nature, I admit, must first have made you capable of adopting them, and then observation and imitation will make them in time your own. There are graces of the mind as well as of the body; the former give an easy, engaging turn to the thoughts and the expressions, the latter to motions, attitude, and address. No man perhaps ever possessed them all; he would be too happy that did: but if you will attentively observe those graceful and engaging manners which please you most in other people, you may easily collect what will equally please others in you and engage the majority of the Graces on your side, insure the casting vote, and be returned *aimable*. There are people whom the *Précieuse* of Molière very justly though very affectedly calls " les Antipodes des Graces." If these unhappy people are formed by nature invincibly *Maussades* and awkward, they are to be pitied rather than blamed or ridiculed; but nature has disinherited few people to that degree.

X.

TRUE WIT AND ITS JUDICIOUS USE.

BATH, *Dec.* 18, 1765.

MY DEAR LITTLE BOY, — If God gives you wit, which I am not sure that I wish you unless He gives you at the same time an equal portion at least of judgment to keep it in good order, wear it like your sword in the scabbard and do not brandish it to the terror of the whole company. If you have real wit it will flow spontaneously, and you need not aim at it, for in that case the rule of the Gospel is reversed, and it will prove, Seek and you shall *not* find. Wit is so shining a quality that everybody admires it, most people aim at it, all people fear it, and few love it unless in themselves. A man must have a good share of wit himself to endure a great share of it in another. When wit exerts itself in satire it is a most malignant distemper; wit it is true may be shown in satire, but satire does not constitute wit, as most fools imagine it does. A man of real wit will find a thousand better occasions of showing it. Abstain therefore most carefully from satire, which though it fall upon no particular person in company and momentarily from the malignity of the human heart pleases all, upon reflection it frightens all too; they think it may be their turn next, and will hate you for what they find you could say of them more than be obliged to you for what you do not say. Fear and hatred are next-door neighbors. The more wit you have the more good nature and politeness you must show, to induce people to pardon your superiority, for that is no easy matter. . . . The character of a man of wit is a shining one that every man would have if he could, though it is often attended by some inconveniencies; the dullest alderman even aims at it, cracks his dull joke, and thinks or at least hopes that it is wit. But the denomination of *a wit* is always formidable and very often ridiculous. These titular *wits* have commonly much less wit than petulance and presumption. They are at best *les rieurs de leur quartier*, in which narrow sphere they are at once feared and admired. You will perhaps ask me, and justly, how, considering the delusions of self love and vanity, from which no man living is absolutely free, how you shall know whether you have wit or not. To which the best answer I can give you is, not to trust to the voice of your own judgment, for it will deceive you; nor to your ears, which will always greedily receive flattery, if you are worth being flattered; but trust only to your eyes, and read in the countenances of good company their approbation or dislike of what you say. Observe carefully too whether you are sought for, solicited, and in a manner pressed into good company. But even all this will not absolutely ascertain your wit, therefore do not upon this encouragement flash your wit in people's faces a *ricochets*, in the shape of *bons mots*, epigrams, smart *reparties*, etc. Have rather less than more wit than you really have. A wise man will live at least as much within his wit as within his income. Content yourself with good sense and reason, which at long run are sure to please everybody who has either. If wit comes into the bargain, welcome it, but never invite it. Bear this truth always in your mind, that you may be admired for your wit if you have any, but that nothing but good sense and good qualities can make you be loved. They are substantial, every day's wear. Wit is for *les jours de gala*, where people go chiefly to be stared at.

. . . .

XI.

RAILLERY, MIMICRY, WAGS, AND WITLINGS.

Dec. 28, 1765.

MY DEAR LITTLE BOY,—There is a species of minor wit which is much used and much more abused,—I mean Raillery. It is a most mischievous and dangerous weapon when in unskilful or clumsy hands, and it is much safer to let it quite alone than to play with it; and yet almost everybody does play with it, though they see daily the quarrels and heart-burnings that it occasions. In truth it implies a supposed superiority in the *railleur* to the *raillé;* which no man likes even the suspicion of in his own case, though it may divert him in other people's. An innocent *raillerie* is often inoffensively begun but very seldom inoffensively ended, for that depends upon the *raillé*, who if he cannot defend himself well grows brutal, and if he can, very possibly his *railleur*, baffled and disappointed, becomes so. It is a sort of trial of wit in which no man can patiently bear to have his inferiority made appear. The character of a *railleur* is more generally feared and more heartily hated than any one I know in the world. The injustice of a bad man is sooner forgiven than the insult of a witty one. The former only hurts one's liberty or property, but the latter hurts and mortifies that secret pride which no human breast is free from. I will allow that there is a sort of raillery which may not only be inoffensive but even flattering, as when by a genteel irony you accuse people of those imperfections which they are most notoriously free from and consequently insinuate that they possess the contrary virtues. You may safely call Aristides a knave, or a very handsome woman an ugly one; but take care that neither the man's character nor the lady's beauty be in the least doubtful. But this sort of raillery requires a very light and steady hand to administer it. A little too rough, it may be mistaken into an offence, and a little too smooth, it may be thought a sneer, which is a most odious thing. There is another sort, I will not call it of wit, but rather of merriment and buffoonry, which is mimicry; the most successful mimic in the world is always the most absurd fellow, and an ape is infinitely his superior. His profession is to imitate and ridicule those natural defects and deformities for which no man is in the least accountable, and in their imitation of them make themselves for the time as disagreeable and shocking as those they mimic. But I will say no more of these creatures, who only amuse the lowest rabble of mankind. There is another sort of human animals called *wags*, whose profession is to make the company laugh immoderately, and who always succeed provided the company consist of fools, but who are greatly disappointed in finding that they never can alter a muscle in the face of a man of sense. This is a most contemptible character and never esteemed, even by those who are silly enough to be diverted by them. Be content both for yourself with sound good sense and good manners, and let wit be thrown into the bargain where it is proper and inoffensive. Good sense will make you be esteemed, good manners be loved, and wit give a lustre to both.

. . . .

XII.

THE COXCOMB.—THE TIMID MAN.

Jan. 2, 1766.

My dear little Boy,—If there is a lawful and proper object of raillery it seems to be a coxcomb, as an usurper of the common rights of mankind. But here some precautions are necessary. Some wit and great presumption constitute a coxcomb, for a true coxcomb must have parts. The most consummate coxcomb I ever knew was a man of the most wit, but whose wit, bloated with presumption, made him too big for any company, where he always usurped the seat of empire and crowded out common sense. *Raillerie* seems to be a proper rod for these offenders, but great caution and skill are necessary in the use of it or you may happen to catch a Tartar as they call it, and then the laughers will be against you. The best way with these people is to let them quite alone and give them rope enough. On the other hand there are many and perhaps more who suffer from their timidity and *mauvaise honte*, which sink them infinitely below their level. Timidity is generally taken for stupidity, which for the most part it is not, but proceeds from a want of education in good company. Mr. Addison was the most timid and awkward man in good company I ever saw, and no wonder, for he had been wholly cloistered up in the cells of Oxford till he was five and twenty years old. La Bruyère says, and there is a great deal of truth in it, "qu'on ne vaut dans ce monde que ce que l'on veut valoir;" for in this respect mankind show great indulgence and value people at pretty near the price they set upon themselves, if it be not exorbitant. I could wish you to have a cool intrepid assurance with great seeming modesty, — never *démonté* and never forward. Very awkward timid people who have not been used to good company are either ridiculously bashful or absurdly impudent. I have known many a man impudent from shamefacedness, endeavoring to act a reasonable assurance and lashing himself up to what he imagines to be a proper and easy behavior. A very timid bashful man is annihilated in good company, especially of his superiors. He does not know what he says or does and is in a ridiculous agitation both of body and mind. Avoid both these extremes and endeavor to possess yourself with coolness and steadiness. Speak to the King with full as little concern (though with more respect) as you would to your equals. This is the distinguishing characteristic of a gentleman and a man of the world. The way to acquire this most necessary behavior is, as I have told you before, to keep company, whatever difficulty it may cost you at first, with your superiors and with women of fashion, instead of taking refuge as too many young people do in low and bad company in order to avoid the restraint of good breeding. It is, I confess, a pretty difficult, not to say an impossible thing, for a young man at his first appearance in the world and unused to the ways and manners of it, not to be disconcerted and embarrassed. When he first comes into what is called the best company, he sees that they stare at him, and if they happen to laugh he is sure that they laugh at him. This awkwardness is not to be blamed, as it often proceeds from laudable causes, from a modest diffidence of himself and a consciousness of not yet knowing the modes and manners of good company; but let him persevere with a becoming modesty and he will find that all people of good nature and good breeding will assist and help him out instead of laughing at him, and then a very little usage of the world and an attentive observation will soon give him a proper knowledge of it. It is the characteristic of low and bad company, which commonly consists of wags and witlings, to laugh at, disconcert, and as they call it bamboozle a young fellow of ingenuous modesty. You will tell me perhaps that to do all this one must have a good share of vanity; I grant it, but the great point is *ne quid nimis*, for I fear that Monsieur de la Rochefoucault's maxim is too true, " que la vertu n'iroit pas loin, si la vanité ne lui tenoit pas compagnie." A man who despairs of pleasing will never please; a man who is sure that he shall always please wherever he goes, is a coxcomb; but the man who hopes and endeavors to please, and believes that he may, will most infallibly please.

XIII.

THE "MAN OF SPIRIT."—SCANDAL AND INSINUATION.

Jan. 10, 1766.

MY DEAR LITTLE BOY,—I know that you are generous and benevolent in your nature, but that, though the principal point, is not quite enough; you must seem so too. I do not mean ostentatiously, but do not be ashamed as many young fellows are of owning the laudable sentiments of good-nature and humanity which you really feel. I have known many young men who desired to be reckoned men of spirit affect a hardness and an unfeelingness which in reality they never had. Their conversation is in the decisive and minatory tone; they are for breaking bones, cutting off ears, throwing people out of the window, etc., and all these fine declarations they ratify with horrible and silly oaths. All this is to be thought men of spirit! Astonishing error this, which necessarily reduces them to this dilemma,— if they really mean what they say, they are brutes, and if they do not, they are fools for saying it. This however is a common character amongst young men. Carefully avoid this contagion and content yourself with being calmly and mildly resolute and steady when you are thoroughly convinced that you are in the right, for this is true spirit. What is commonly called in the world a man or a woman of spirit, are the two most detestable and most dangerous animals that inhabit it. They are wrongheaded, captious, jealous, offended without reason and offending with as little. The man of spirit has immediate recourse to his sword and the woman of spirit to her tongue, and it is hard to say which of the two is the most mischievous weapon. It is too usual a thing in many companies to take the tone of scandal and defamation; some gratify their malice and others think that they show their wit by it. But I hope that you will never adopt this tone. On the contrary do you always take the favorable side of the question, and, without an offensive and flat contradiction, seem to doubt, and represent the uncertainty of reports, where private malice is at least very apt to mingle itself. This candid and temperate behavior will please the whole uncandid company, though a sort of gentle contradiction to their unfavorable insinuations, as it makes them hope that they may in their turns find an advocate in you. There is another kind of offensiveness often used in company, which is to throw out hints and insinuations only applicable to and felt by one or two persons in the company, who are consequently both embarrassed and angry, and the more so as they are the more unwilling to show that they apply these hints to themselves. Have a watch over yourself never to say anything that either the whole company or any one person in it can reasonably or probably take ill, and remember the French saying, "qu'il ne faut pas parler de corde dans la maison d'un pendu." Good-nature universally charms even all those who have none, and it is impossible to be *aimable* without both the reality and the appearances of it.

XIV.

VANITY. — FEIGNED SELF-CONDEMNATION.

Jan. 14, 1766.

MY DEAR LITTLE BOY, — The *Egotism* is the usual and favorite figure of most people's rhetoric, which I hope you will never adopt, but on the contrary most scrupulously avoid. Nothing is more disagreeable nor irksome to the company than to hear a man either praising or condemning himself: for both proceed from the same motive, vanity. I would allow no man to speak of himself unless in a Court of Justice in his own defence, or as a witness. Shall a man speak in his own praise, however justly? No. The hero of his own little tale always puzzles and disgusts the company, who do not know what to say nor how to look. Shall he blame himself? No. Vanity is as much the motive of his self-condemnation as of his own panegyric. I have known many people take shame to themselves, and with a modest contrition confess themselves guilty of most of the cardinal virtues. They have such a weakness in their nature that they cannot help being too much moved with the misfortunes and miseries of their fellow-creatures, which they feel perhaps more but at least as much as they do their own. Their generosity, they are sensible, is imprudence, for they are apt to carry it too far, from the weak though irresistible beneficence of their nature. They are possibly too jealous of their honor, and too irascible whenever they think that it is touched ; and this proceeds from their unhappy warm constitution, which makes them too tender and sensible upon that point. And so on of all the virtues possible. A poor trick, and a wretched instance of human vanity that defeats its own purpose. Do you be sure never to speak of yourself, for yourself, nor against yourself; but let your character speak for you. Whatever that says will be believed, but whatever you say of it will not, and only make you odious or ridiculous. Be constantly upon your guard against the various snares and effects of vanity and self-love. It is impossible to extinguish them ; they are without exception in every human breast, and in the present state of nature it is very right that they should be so ; but endeavor to keep them within due bounds, which is very possible. In this case dissimulation is almost meritorious, and the seeming modesty of the hero or of the patriot adorns their other virtues ; I use the word of "seeming," for their *valets de chambre* know better. Vanity is the more odious and shocking to everybody, because everybody without exception has vanity; and two vanities can never love one another, any more than according to the vulgar saying, two of a trade can.

. . . .

XV.

ATTENTION. — THE SENSE OF PROPRIETY.

Jan. 21, 1766.

My dear little Boy, — I have more than once recommended to you in the course of our correspondence *Attention*, but I shall frequently recur to that subject, which is as inexhaustible as it is important. Attend carefully in the first place to human nature in general, which is pretty much the same in all human creatures and varies chiefly by modes, habits, education, and example. Analyze, and if I may use the expression, anatomize it. Study your own, and that will lead you to know other people's. Carefully observe the words, the looks, and gestures of the whole company you are in, and retain all their little singularities, humors, tastes, antipathies, and affections, which will enable you to please or avoid them occasionally as your judgment may direct you. I will give you the most trifling instance of this that can be imagined, and yet will be sure to please. If you invite anybody to dinner you should take care to provide those things which you have observed them to like more particularly, and not to have those things which you know they have an antipathy to. These trifling things go a great way in the art of pleasing, and the more so from being so trifling that they are flattering proofs of your regard for the persons even to *minucies*. These things are what the French call *des attentions*, which (to do them justice) they study and practise more than any people in Europe. Attend to and look at whoever speaks to you; and never seem *distrait* or *rêveur*, as if you did not hear them at all, for nothing is more contemptuous and consequently more shocking. It is true you will by these means often be obliged to attend to things not worth anybody's attention, but it is a necessary sacrifice to be made to good manners in society. A minute attention is also necessary to time, place, and characters. A *bon mot* in one company is not so in another, but on the contrary may prove offensive. Never joke with those whom you observe to be at that time pensive and grave; and on the other hand do not preach and moralize in a company full of mirth and gayety. Many people come into company full of what they intend to say in it themselves without the least regard to others, and thus charged up to the muzzle are resolved to let it off at any rate. I knew a man who had a story about a gun which he thought a good one and that he told it very well; he tried all means in the world to turn the conversation upon guns, but if he failed in his attempt he started in his chair and said he heard a gun fired, but when the company assured him that they heard no such thing, he answered, " Perhaps then I was mistaken but however, since we are talking of guns; " — and then told his story, to the great indignation of the company. Become, as far as with innocence and honor you can, all things to all men, and you will gain a great many. Have *des prevenances* to, and say or do what you judge beforehand will be most agreeable to them without their hinting at or expecting it. It would be endless to specify the numberless opportunities that every man has of pleasing if he will but make use of them. Your own good sense will suggest them to you, and your good-nature and even your interest will induce you to practise them. Great attention is to be had to times and seasons; for example, at meals, talk often but never long at a time, for the frivolous bustle of the servants, and often the more frivolous conversation of the guests, which chiefly turns upon kitchen-stuff and cellar-stuff, will not bear any long reasonings or relations. Meals are and were always reckoned the moments of relaxation of the mind, and sacred to easy mirth and social cheerfulness. Conform to this custom and furnish your quota of good-humor, but be not induced by example to the frequent excess of gluttony or intemperance. The former inevitably produces dulness, the latter madness. Observe the *à propos* in everything you say or do. In conversing with those who are much your superiors, however easy and familiar you may and ought to be with them, preserve the respect that is due to them. Converse with your equals with an easy familiarity and at the same time with great civility and decency. But too much familiarity, according to the old saying, often breeds contempt and sometimes quarrels; and I know nothing more difficult in common behavior than to fix due bounds to familiarity; too little implies an unsociable formality, too much destroys all friendly and social intercourse. The best rule I can give you to manage familiarity, is never to be more familiar with anybody than you would be willing and even glad that he should be with you ; on the other hand avoid that uncomfortable reserve and coldness which is generally the shield of cunning, or the protection of dulness. The Italian maxim is a wise one, " Volto sciolto e pensieri stretti ; " that is, let your countenance be open, and your thoughts be close. To your inferiors you should use a hearty benevolence in your words and actions instead of a refined politeness which would be apt to make them suspect that you rather laughed at them. For example, you must show civility to a mere country gentleman in a very different manner from what you do to a man of the world. Your reception of him should seem hearty and rather coarse to relieve him from the embarrassment of his own *mauvaise honte*. Have attention even in company of fools, for though they are fools they may perhaps drop or repeat something worth your knowing and which you may profit by. Never talk your best in the company of fools, for they would not understand you, and would perhaps suspect that you jeered them, as they commonly call it ; but talk only the plainest common-sense to them, and very gravely, for there is no jesting nor *badinage* with them. Upon the whole with attention and *les attentions* you will be sure to please ; without them you will be as sure to offend.

XVI.

AFFECTATIONS. — POLITE CONVERSATION.

[*No Date.*]

My dear little Boy, — Carefully avoid all affectation either of mind or body. It is a very true and a very trite observation that no man is ridiculous for being what he really is, but for affecting to be what he is not. No man is awkward by nature, but by affecting to be genteel; and I have known many a man of common-sense pass generally for a fool, because he affected a degree of wit that God had denied him. A ploughman is by no means awkward in the exercise of his trade, but would be exceedingly ridiculous if he attempted the air and graces of a man of fashion. You learned to dance, but it was not for the sake of dancing, but it was to bring your air and motions back to what they would naturally have been if they had had fair play, and had not been warped in your youth by bad examples and awkward imitations of other boys. Nature may be cultivated and improved both as to the body and as to the mind; but it is not to be extinguished by art, and all endeavors of that kind are absurd, and an inexhaustible fund for ridicule. Your body and mind must be at ease to be agreeable; but affectation is a perpetual constraint under which no man can be genteel in his carriage or pleasing in his conversation. Do you think that your motions would be easy or graceful if you wore the clothes of another man much slenderer or taller than yourself?

Certainly not; it is the same thing with the mind, if you affect a character that does not fit you, and that Nature never intended for you. But here do not mistake and think that it follows from hence that you should exhibit your whole character to the public because it is your natural one. No; many things must be suppressed, and many occasionally concealed in the best character. Never force Nature, but it is by no means necessary to show it all. Here discretion must come to your assistance, that sure and safe guide through life,— discretion, that necessary companion to reason, and the useful *garde-fou*, if I may use that expression, to wit and imagination. Discretion points out the *à propos*, the *decorum*, the *ne quid nimis;* and will carry a man of moderate parts further than the most shining parts would without it. It is another word for "judgment," though not quite synonymous to it. Judgment is not upon all occasions required, but discretion always is. Never affect nor assume a particular character, for it will never fit you, but will probably give you a ridicule; but leave it to your conduct, your virtues, your morals, and your manners to give you one. Discretion will teach you to have particular attention to your *mœurs*, which we have no one word in our language to express exactly. "Morals" are too much, "manners" too little; "decency" comes the nearest to it, though rather short of it. Cicero's word "decorum" is properly the thing, and I see no reason why that expressive word should not be adopted and naturalized in our language; I have never scrupled using it in that sense. *À propos* of words, study your own language more carefully than most English people do. Get a habit of speaking it with propriety and elegancy. For there are few things more disagreeable than to hear a gentleman talk the barbarisms, the solecisms, and the vulgarisms of porters. Avoid, on the other hand, a stiff and formal accuracy, especially what the women call "hard words," when plain ones as expressive are at hand. The French make it a study to "bien narrer," and to say the truth they are apt to "narrer trop," and with too affected an elegancy. The three commonest topics of conversation are religion, politics, and news. All people think that they understand the two first perfectly, though they never studied either, and are therefore very apt to talk of them both dogmatically and ignorantly, consequently with warmth. But religion is by no means a proper subject for conversation in a mixed company. It should only be treated among a very few people of learning for mutual instruction. It is too awful and respectable a subject to become a familiar one. Therefore never mingle yourself in it, any further than to express a universal toleration and indulgence to all errors in it, if conscientiously entertained; for every man has as good a right to think as he does as you have to think as you do; nay, in truth he cannot help it. As for politics, they are still more universally understood, and as every one thinks his private interest more or less concerned in them, nobody hesitates to pronounce decisively upon them, not even the ladies; . the copiousness of whose eloquence is more to be admired upon that subject than the conclusiveness of their logic. It will be impossible for you to avoid engaging in these conversations, for there are hardly any others; but take care to do it very coolly and with great good-humor; and whenever you find that the company begins to be heated and noisy for the good of their country, be only a patient hearer; unless you can interpose by some agreeable *badinage* and restore good-humor to the company. And here I cannot help observing to you that nothing is more useful either to put off or to parry disagreeable and puzzling affairs, than a good-humored and genteel *badinage*. I have found it so by long experience, but this *badinage* must not be carried to *mauvaise plaisanterie*. It must be light without being frivolous, sensible without being in the least sententious, and in short have that pleasing *je ne sais quoi*, which everybody feels, and nobody can describe.

XVII.

EPITAPH ON A WIFE.

BLACK-HEATH, *Mercredi*, 4 *Juin* [1766].

MON CHER PETIT DRÔLE, — Ne négligeons pas le François, qu'il faut que vous sachiez parler et écrire corréctement et avec elégance. Un honnête homme doit scavoir l'Anglois et le François également bien, l'Anglois parceque c'est votre propre langue, et que ce seroit honteux d'en ignorer même les minucies, et le François parceque c'est en quelque façon la langue universelle. Voicy donc un epitaphe que fit un homme sur la mort de sa femme, qui lui étoit fort incommode et dont il étoit fort las.

> Cy git ma femme, Ah! qu'elle est bien
> Pour son repos et pour le mien.

. . . .

XVIII.

EVERY MAN THE ARCHITECT OF HIS OWN FORTUNE.

BLACK-HEATH, *Aug.* 26, 1766.

MY DEAR LITTLE BOY,—Your French letter was a very good one, considering how long you have been disused to write in that language. There are indeed some few faults in it, which I will show you when we meet next, for I keep your letter by me for that purpose. One cannot correct one's faults without knowing them, and I always looked upon those who told me of mine as friends, instead of being displeased or angry, as people in general are too apt to be. You say that I laugh at you when I tell you that you may very probably in time be Secretary of State. No, I am very serious in saying that you may if you please, if you take the proper methods to be so. Writing well and speaking well in public are the necessary qualifications for it, and they are very easily acquired by attention and application. In all events, aim at it; and if you do not get it, let it be said of you what was said of Phaethon, "Magnis tamen excidit ausis."

Every man of a generous, noble spirit desires

first to please and then to shine; *Facere digna scribi vel scribere digna legi.* Fools and indolent people lay all their disappointments to the charge of their ill fortune, but there is no such thing as good or ill fortune. Every man makes his own fortune in proportion to his merit. An ancient author whom you are not yet, but will in time be, acquainted with says very justly, "Nullum numen abest si sit prudentia; nos te fortuna Deam facimus caeloque locamus." Prudence there means those qualifications and that conduct that will command fortune. Let that be your motto and have it always in your mind. I was sure that you would soon come to like your voluntary study, and I will appeal to yourself, could you employ that hour more agreeably? And is it not better than what thoughtless boys of your age commonly call play, which is running about without any object or design and only *pour tuer le temps? Faire des riens* is the most miserable abuse and loss of time that can possibly be imagined. You must know that I have in the main a great opinion of you; therefore take great care and pains not to forfeit it. And so God bless you. *Non progredi est regredi.*

XIX.

INATTENTION. — *HOC AGE*

BLACK-HEATH, *Oct.* 4, 1766.

MY DEAR LITTLE BOY, — *Amoto quaeramus seria ludo.* I have often trifled with you in my letters and there is no harm in trifling sometimes. Dr. Swift used often to say, "Vive la bagatelle," but everything has its proper season; and when I consider your age now it is proper, I think, to be sometimes serious. You know I love you mightily, and I find but one single fault with you. You are the best-natured boy; you have good parts and an excellent memory; but now to your fault, which you may so easily correct that I am astonished that your own good sense does not make you do it. It is your giddiness and inattention which you confessed to me. You know that without a good stock of learning you can never, when you are a man, be received in good company; and the only way to acquire that stock is to apply with attention and diligence to whatever you are taught. The *hoc age* is of the utmost consequence in every part of life. No man can do or think of two things at a time to any purpose, and whoever does two things at once is sure to do them both ill. It is the characteristic of a futile, frivolous man to be doing one thing and at the same time thinking of another. Do not imagine that I would have you plod and study all day long; no, leave that to dull boys. On the contrary I would have you divert yourself and be as gay as ever you please; but while you are learning, mind that only, and think of nothing else; it will be the sooner over. They tell an idle story of Julius Caesar that he dictated to six secretaries at once and upon different businesses. This I am sure is as false as it is absurd, for Caesar had too good sense to do any two things at once. I am sure that for the future you will attend diligently to whatever you are doing, and that for two reasons; the one is that your own good sense at eleven years old will show you not only the utility but the necessity of learning, the other is that if you love me as I believe you do, you will cheerfully do what I so earnestly ask of you for your own sake only. When I see you next, which shall not be very long, first I flatter myself that the Doctor will give me a very good account of your close attention. Good-night.

XX.

THE PRIDE OF RANK AND BIRTH.

BATH, *Nov.* 5, 1766.

MY DEAR LITTLE BOY, — See how punctual I am; I told you that I would write to you first from hence; I arrived here but yesterday, and I write to-day. When I saw you last Sunday you assured me that you had a clear conscience; and I believe it, for I cannot suppose you could be guilty of so horrible a crime as that of asserting an untruth. To say the truth I think you have but few faults; and as I perceive them I shall make it my business to correct them, and assume the office of censor. If I mistake not, I have discovered in that little heart some lurking seeds of pride, which nature, who has been very kind to you, never sowed there, but were transplanted there by vulgar folly and adulation at Mansfield. You were there my Young Squire, and sometimes, perhaps, by anticipation my

Young Lord. Well, and what then? Do not you feel that you owe those advantages wholly to chance, and not to any merit of your own? Are you better born, as silly people call it, than the servant who wipes your shoes? Not in the least; he had a father and a mother, and they had fathers and mothers and grandfathers and grandmothers and so on, up to the first creation of the human species, and is consequently of as ancient a family as yourself.[1] It is true your family has been more lucky than his, but not one jot better. You will find in Ulysses's speech for the armor of Achilles this sensible observation: "Nam genus et proavos, et quae non fecimus ipsi vix ea nostra voco."

Moreover you desire, and very laudably, to please; which if you have any pride is absolutely impossible, for there is not in nature so hateful and so ridiculous a character as that of a man who is proud of his birth and rank. All people hate and ridicule him; he is mimicked and has nick-names given him, such as "the Sovereign," "the Sublime," "the Stately," etc. I allow you to be proud of superior merit and learning when you have them, but that is not the blameable and absurd pride of birth

---

[1] There is a story illustrative of this passage and characteristic of Lord Chesterfield's humor. A picture of a man and woman and two boys with the Stanhope Arms in the corner was given by some one to Lord Chesterfield, as an evidence of family antiquity. He accepted the gift and wrote under it, "Adam Stanhope of Eden Garden and Eve Stanhope his wife, with their two sons, Cain Stanhope and Abel Stanhope." See Mrs. Carter's Letters from 1741 to 1770, i. 32. — EARL OF CARNARVON: *Memoir of Chesterfield.*

and rank that I mean ; on the contrary, it is a blameless and pardonable vanity, if not carried too far.

. . . .

XXI.

SHINING THOUGHTS OF ANCIENT AND MODERN
AUTHORS.

Saturday Morning [*January*, 1767].

My Dear Boy, —

. . . .

I send you a book which I think must gratify your love of variety. It is a collection of the most shining thoughts both of the ancients and of the moderns, compiled by the famous Père Bouhours, a Jesuit, a man of great parts and sound judgment. I endeavor to stock your mind with the most ingenious thoughts of other people, in hopes that they may suggest to you materials for thinking yourself; for an honest man will no more live upon the credit of other people's thoughts than of their fortune. When, therefore, you dip into this book, and that any thought pleases you much, ask yourself why it pleases you, and examine whether it is founded upon truth and nature, for nothing else can please at long run. Tinsel false thoughts may impose upon one for a short time, like false money ; but sterling coin alone will always and everywhere pass current. God bless you and make you both an honest and an able man, but the former above all things.

XXII.

AVARICE AND AMBITION.

Monday Morning [*March*, 1767].

MY DEAR BOY, — I was very glad to hear that in one of your late essays you preferred ambition to avarice, and indeed there is hardly any comparison between them. Avarice is a mean, ignoble, and dirty passion; I never knew a miser that had any one great or good quality; but ambition, even where it is a vice, is at least the vice of a gentleman. Ambition, according to its object, is either blamable or commendable. Tyrants and conquerors, who ravage and desolate the world, and trample upon all the rights of mankind to gratify their ambition, are doubtless the greatest and most dangerous of all criminals. But an ambition to excel others in all virtuous and laudable things is not only blameless, but highly meritorious, and should extend from the least to the greatest objects. You may and I hope have that ambition in your little sphere. I remember that when I was of your age, I had a strong ambition to excel all my contemporaries in whatever was praiseworthy. I labored hard to outstrip them in learning; I was mortified if in our little plays they seemed more dexterous than I was; nay, I was uneasy if they danced, walked, or sat more genteelly than myself. Those little things are by no means to be neglected, for they are of more use in the common intercourse of life than you imagine them to be, especially in your profession, which is speaking in public. I say in your *profession*, for you must excel in that or you will be nobody. You guess, I am sure, that I mean speaking well, both in public assemblies and in private conversation. Cicero speaks of eloquence as the principal object of a laudable ambition, and asserts it to be the chief distinction between man and beast. " Quam ob rem quis hoc non jure miretur, summeque in eo elaborandum esse arbitretur, ut, quo uno homines maxime bestiis praestent, in hoc hominibus ipsis antecellat." This is one kind of ambition, whose object is pleasure and public utility, and consequently meritorious. Oh, what exquisite joy must it give an honest man (you see I endeavor to imitate your florid eloquence) to see multitudes hang upon his tongue, and persuaded to adopt his opinion instead of their own ! — if they had any, for very often they have none, and if they have, it is probably an erroneous one. I send you herewith an excellent collection of Cicero's thoughts upon various subjects, the Latin on one side, and the French translation by L.'Abbé d'Olivet on the other, which French translation will enable you to understand the original Latin better than can be expected at your age. I have marked what he says upon eloquence; read it with attention. God bless my boy.

XXIII.

THE ENDEAVOR TO ATTAIN PERFECTION.—SPORTING TASTES.

BATH, *Nov.* 17, 1767.

MY DEAR LITTLE BOY,—Your last letter was so good a one that had it not been for Dr. Dodd's attestation that it was all your own, I should have thought it a translation of one of Cicero's or Pliny's, those two acknowledged standards of epistolary perfection. However, go on, and strive to attain to absolute perfection in writing, as in everything else that you do; for though absolute perfection is denied to human nature, those who take the most pains to arrive at it will come the nearest to it. The famous disturber and scourge of mankind, Charles the Twelfth of Sweden, in his low camp style used to say that by resolution and perseverance a man might do everything. . . . I own I cannot entirely agree with his Swedish Majesty; but so much I will venture to say, that every man may by unremitting application and endeavors, do much more than at the first setting out he thought it possible that he ever could do. Learn to distinguish between difficulties and impossibilities, which many people do not. The silly and the sanguine look upon impossibilities to be only difficulties; as on the other hand the lazy and the timorous take every difficulty for an impossibility. A greater knowledge of the world will teach you the proper medium between those two extremes. I approve greatly of your father's method of shooting his game with his pen only, and heartily wish that when you have game of your own you may use no other. For my part I never in my life killed my own meat, but left it to the poulterer and butcher to do it for me. All those country sports, as they are called, are the effects of the ignorance and idleness of country esquires, who do not know what to do with their time; but people of sense and knowledge never give in to those illiberal amusements. You make me fair promises in your letter of what you will do; but remember that at the same time you give me great claims upon you, for I look upon your promises to be engagements upon the word and honor of a gentleman, which I hope you will never violate upon this or any other occasion. I have long ago and often repeated to you "qu'un homme d'honneur n'a que sa parole." God bless you.

My compliments to your whole house.

XXIV.

THE TREATMENT OF INFERIORS.

BLACK-HEATH, *Tuesday.*

MY DEAR BOY, — You behaved yourself last Saturday very much like a gentleman, and better than any boy in England of your age would or could have done. Go on so, and when you are a man you will be with more acquaintance with the world and good company what I most earnestly wish you to be, the best bred and consequently the best liked gentleman in England. Good breeding, and a certain *suavitas morum*, shines and charms in every situation of life with relation to all sorts and ranks of people, as well the lowest as the highest. There is a degree of good breeding towards those who are greatly your inferiors which is in truth common humanity and good-nature; and yet I have known some persons who in other respects were well bred brutal to their servants and dependents. This is mean, and implies a hardness of heart, and is what I am sure you never will be guilty of. When you use the imperative mood to your servants or dependents, who are your equals by nature (and only your inferiors by the malice of their fortune), you will add some softening word, such as "pray do so and so," or " I wish you would do so." You cannot conceive how much that *suavity* of manners will endear you to everybody, even to those who have it not themselves. In high life there are a thousand *minucies* of good breeding which though *minucies* in themselves are so necessary and agreeable as to deserve your utmost attention and imitation, — as for instance what the French call " le bon ton " or " le ton de la bonne compagnie," by which is meant the fashionable tone of good company. This consists of many trifling articles in themselves which when cast up and added together make a total of infinite consequence.

Observe and adopt all those little graces and modes of the best company. Suppose two men of equal abilities employed in the same business, but one of them perfectly well bred and engaging, and the other with only the common run of civility; the former will certainly succeed much better and sooner than the latter.

. . . .

XXV.

THE FALSE PRIDE OF RANK.

BLACK-HEATH, *July* 16, 1768.

I dare say you know, and perhaps too well, that in time probably you will have a title and a good estate; but I dare say you know too that you will owe them merely to chance and not to any merit of your own, be your merit never so great. Whenever you come to the possession of them, there will be people enough mean and absurd enough to flatter you upon them. Be upon your guard against such wretches, and be assured that they must think you a fool and that they have private views to gratify by such impudent adulation. The most absurd character that I know of in the world, and the finest food for satire and ridicule, is a sublime and stately man of quality, who without one grain of any merit struts pompously in all the dignity of an ancient descent *from a long, restive race of droning kings*, or more probably derived to him from fool to fool. I could name many men of great quality and fortune who would pass through the world quietly, unknown and unlaughed at, were it not for those accidental advantages upon which they value themselves and treat their inferiors, as they call them, with arrogance and contempt. But I never knew a man of quality and fortune respected upon those accounts unless he was humble with his title, and extensively generous and beneficent with his fortune. "My Lord" is become a ridiculous nick-name for those proud fools, — "See, My Lord comes," "There's My Lord;" that is, in other words, "See the puppy," "There is the blockhead." I am sure you would by all means avoid ridicule, for it sticks longer even than an injury; and to avoid it, wear your title as if you had it not; but for your estate, let distress and want even without merit feel that you have one. I remember four fine lines of Voltaire upon this subject: —

> "Repandez vos bienfaits avec magnificence,
> Même aux moins vertueux ne les refusez pas;
> Ne vous informez pas de leur reconnoissance,
> Il est grand, il est beau, de faire des ingrats."

By these virtues you may dignify your title when you have one, but remember that your title without them can never dignify you. Nothing is more common than pride without dignity. A man of sense and virtue will always have dignity; but a fool, if shuffled by chance into great rank and fortune, will be proud of both. There is as much difference between pride and dignity as there is between power and authority. Power may fall to the share of a Nero or a Caligula, but authority can only be the attendant of the confidence mankind have in your sense and virtue. Aristides and Cato had authority.

• • • • • • • • • •

XXVI.

THE STRICT VERACITY OF A GENTLEMAN.

BLACK-HEATH, *July* 30, 1768.

MY DEAR BOY, — My two objects in your education are and always have been to give you learning enough to distinguish yourself in Parliament, and manners to shine in courts. The former is in the best hands, Dr. Dodd's; but the latter department I shall undertake myself, from my long experience and knowledge of the ways of the world. I am sure you would be a gentleman, and I am as sure that I would by all means have you one. "A gentleman" is a complex term, answers exactly to the French word "honnête homme," and comprehends manners, decorum, politeness, but above all strict veracity; for without that all the accomplishments in the world avail nothing. A man who is once detected in a lie — and every liar is sooner or later detected — is irrecoverably sunk into infamy. Nobody will believe him afterwards even upon his oath. To tell a man that he lies is the greatest affront that can be offered him, and according to the mad but indispensable custom of the world, can only be washed off by blood. If a man gives another the lie, though ever so justly, what must the liar do? He must fight him, and so justify one crime by (if possible) a greater, — a chance of murdering or of being murdered; and this is what every one who deviates from truth is sooner or later exposed to.

Besides all this there is a moral turpitude in a lie which no palliatives can excuse; and a plain proof of the infamy of this practice is that no man, not even the worst man living, will own himself a liar, though many will own as great crimes. Some people excuse themselves to themselves by only adding to and embellishing truth in their narrations, but falsehood never can be innocent, for it can only be intended to mislead and deceive. But I am sure I have dwelt too long upon this subject to you, who I am persuaded have a just horror for a lie of any kind, or else I should have a horror for you.

I have often recommended to you the good breeding and the manners of a gentleman, and to my great comfort, not without success, for you are in general civil and well bred; the article in which you fail the most is at meals. You eat with too much avidity, and cram your mouth so full that if you were to speak you must sputter the contents of it amongst the dishes and the company. You sometimes eat off of your knife, which is never to be done, and sometimes you play with your knife, fork, or spoon, too, like a boy. These are but little faults, I confess, but however are better corrected than persevered in. In the main it goes very well and I love you mightily. God bless you.

XXVII.

ON THE *JE NE SAIS QUOI*.

BLACK-HEATH, *Aug.* 9, 1768.

MY DEAR BOY, — I dare say you have heard and read of the *je ne sais quoi*,[1] both in French and English, for the expression is now adopted into our language; but I question whether you have any clear idea of it, and indeed it is more easily felt than defined. It is a most inestimable quality, and adorns every other. I will endeavor to give you a general notion of it, though I cannot an exact one; experience must teach it you, and will if you attend to it. It is in my opinion a compound of all the agreeable qualities of body and mind, in which no one of them predominates in such a manner as to give exclusion to any other. It is not mere wit, mere beauty, mere learning, nor indeed mere any one thing that produces it, though they all contribute something towards it. It is owing to this *je ne sais quoi* that one takes a liking to some one particular person at first rather than to another. One feels oneself prepossessed in favor of that person without being enough acquainted with him to judge of his intrinsic merit or talents, and one finds oneself inclined to suppose him to have good sense, good-nature, and good-humor. A genteel

---

[1] It would be difficult to find anything on such a subject where the touch is lighter, the turn of expression happier, and the distinctions more delicately drawn. — EARL OF CARNARVON :- *Memoir of Chesterfield.*

address, graceful motions, a pleasing elocution, and elegancy of style are powerful ingredients in this compound. It is in short an extract of all the "Graces." Here you will perhaps ask me to define the "Graces," which I can only do by the "je ne sais quoi," as I can only define the "je ne sais quoi" by the "Graces." No one person possesses them all, but happy he who possesses the most, and wretched he who possesses none of them. I can much more easily describe what their contraries are, — as for example a head sunk in between the shoulders, feet turned inwards instead of outwards, the manner of walking or rather waddling of a mackaw, so as to make Mrs. Dodd very justly call you her mackaw. All these sort of things are most notorious insults upon the Graces and indeed upon all good company. Do not take into your head that these things are trifles; though they may seem so if singly and separately considered, yet when considered aggregately and relatively to the great and necessary art of pleasing, they are of infinite consequence. Socrates, the wisest and honestest pagan that ever lived, thought the Graces of such vast importance that he always advised his disciples to "sacrifice to them." From so great an authority I will most earnestly recommend to you to sacrifice to them. Invite, entreat, supplicate them to accompany you, in all you say or do; and sacrifice to them every little idle humor and laziness. They will then be propitious, and accept and reward your offerings. The principal object of my few remaining years is to make you perfect, if human nature could be so; and it would make me happy if you would give me reason to say in time of you, what Lucretius says of Memmius: —

"Quem tu Dea tempore in omni,
Omnibus ornatum voluisti excellere rebus."

Turn out your right foot, raise your head above your shoulders, walk like a gentleman; if not I know not what Mrs. Dodd intends to do to you. God bless thee.

XXVIII.

THE INDECENT OSTENTATION OF VICES.

BLACK-HEATH, *Sept.* 3, 1768.

MY DEAR BOY, — You are now near that age in which imitation is not only natural, but in some degree necessary. You are too young to be able to form yourself, and yet you are of an age when you should begin to be forming. Your greatest difficulty will be to choose good models to work from, and I am sorry to tell you that there are at least twenty very bad ones to one good one, especially amongst the youth of the present times. Their manners are illiberal and even their vices are degraded by their indecent ostentation of them. When you come more into the world, be very cautious what model you choose; or rather choose no one singly, but pick and cull the accomplishments of many, as Apelles or Praxiteles, I have forgot which, did to form his celebrated Venus, — not from any one beauty, but by singling out and uniting the best features of a great many. When you hear of any young man, of an universal good character, observe him attentively, and in great measure imitate him; I say in a great measure, for no man living is so perfect as to deserve imitation in every particular. When you hear of another whose good breeding and address are generally applauded, form yourself upon his model in those particulars. Ill examples are sometimes useful to deter from the vices that characterize them. Horace tells us that his father trained him up to virtue by pointing out to him the turpitude of the vices of several individuals.

. . . .

XXIX.

THE ART OF LETTER-WRITING.

BLACK-HEATH, *Sept.* 15, 1768.

MY DEAR BOY, — I send you enclosed a letter from your friend young Mr. Chenevix, which you should answer in about a month. Politeness is as much concerned in answering letters within a reasonable time as it is in returning a bow immediately. À *propos* of letters, let us consider the various kinds of letters, and the general rules concerning them. Letters of business must be answered immediately, and are the easiest either to write or to answer, for the subject is ready and only requires great clearness and perspicuity in the treating. There must be no prettinesses, no quaintnesses, no antitheses, nor even wit. *Non est his locus.* The letters that are the hardest to write are those that are upon no subject at all, and which are like *small talk* in conversation. They admit of wit if you have any, and of agreeable trifling or *badinage*. For as they are nothing in themselves, their whole merit turns upon their ornaments; but they should seem easy and natural, and not smell of the lamp, as most of the letters I have seen printed do, and probably because they were wrote in the intention of printing them. Letters between real intimate friends are of course frequent, but then they require no care nor trouble, for there the heart leaves the understanding little or nothing to do. Matter and expression present themselves. There are two other sorts of letters, but both pretty much of the same nature. These are letters to great men, your superiors, and *lettres galantes* — I do not mean love letters — to fine women. Put flattery enough in them both, and they will be sure to please. I can assure you that men, especially great men, are not in the least behindhand with women in their love of flattery. Whenever you write to persons greatly your inferiors, and by way of giving orders, let your letters speak what I hope in God you will always feel, — the utmost gentleness and humanity. If you happen to write to your *valet de chambre* or your bailiff, it is no great trouble to say " Pray do such a thing;" it will be taken kindly, and your orders will be the better executed for it. What good heart would roughly exert the power and superiority which chance more than merit has given him over many of his fellow creatures? I pray God to bless you, but remember at the same time that probably he will only bless you in proportion to your deserts.

XXX.

TREATMENT OF SERVANTS.

BLACK-HEATH, *Aug.* 29, 1769.

My DEAR BOY, — It gave me great pleasure to observe the indignation which you expressed at the brutality of the Pacha you lately dined with to his servant, which I am sure you are and ever will be incapable of. Those Pachas seem to think that their servants and themselves are not made of the same clay, but that God has made by much the greatest part of mankind to be the oppressed and abused slaves of the superior ranks. Service is a mutual contract, — the master hires and pays his servant, the servant is to do his master's business; but each is equally at liberty to be off of the engagement upon due warning. Servants are full as necessary to their masters as their masters are to them, and so in truth is the whole human species to each other; God has connected them by reciprocal wants and conveniences which must or at least ought to create that sentiment of universal benevolence or good-will which is called *humanity*. Consider were you the only living creature upon this globe what a wretched, miserable being you must be. Where would you get food or clothes? You are full as much obliged to the ploughman for your bread as the ploughman is to you for his wages. In this state then of mutual and universal dependence, what a monster of brutality and injustice must that man be who, though of the highest rank, can treat his fellow creatures even of the lowest with insult and cruelty as if they were of a different and inferior species. But this exhortation is not necessary to you, for I thank God he has given you a good and tender heart; but I would have your benevolence proceed equally from a sense of your duty both to God and man as from the compassionate sentiments and feelings of your heart. Say often to yourself, "Homo sum, nihil humani a me alienum puto." I will encroach no longer upon Dr. Dodd's province, who can and will explain the whole duty of man to you much better than I can; so God bless you, my dear boy.

XXXI.

PRIDE OF RANK AND BIRTH.

BLACK-HEATH, *Sept.* 12, 1769.

MY DEAR BOY, — After my death, Sir William's, and your father's, you will be in a situation that would make a fool proud and insolent, and a wise man more humble and obliging. I therefore easily judge of the effect which it will have upon you. You will have a pretty good estate, and a pretty ancient title. I allow you to be glad of both, but I charge you to be proud of neither of those merely fortuitous advantages, the attendants of your birth, not the rewards of any merit of yours. Your title will enable you to serve your country, your estate to serve your friends, and to realize your present benevolence of heart into beneficence to your fellow creatures. The rabble — that is, at least three parts in four of mankind — admire riches and titles so much that they envy and consequently hate the possessors of them; but if (which too seldom happens) those riches are attended by an extensive beneficence, and the titles by an easy affability, the possessors will then be adored. Take your choice; I am sure you will not hesitate. There is not in my mind a finer subject for ridicule than a man who is proud of his birth and jealous of his rank; his civility is an insolent protection, his walk is stately and processional, and he calls his inferiors only " fellows." I remember a silly lord of this kind who one day, when the House was up, came to the door in Palace Yard, and finding none of his servants there, asked the people who stood at the door, " Where are my fellows;" upon which one of them answered him, " Your lordship has no fellow in the world." All silly men are not proud, but I aver that all proud men are silly without exception. Vanity is not always pride, but pride is always a foolish, ill-grounded vanity. Vanity that arises from a consciousness of virtue and knowledge is a very pardonable vanity, but then even that vanity should be prudently concealed. Upon the whole, the greater your rank, the greater your fortune may be, the more affability, complaisance, and beneficence will be expected from you, if you would not be hated or ridiculous. But I need not I am sure have treated this subject, for your own good sense and good heart would have suggested to you all I have said, and more. God bless you.

XXXII.

THE SNARES OF YOUTH.

Tuesday, June 19, [1770].[1]

MY DEAR BOY, — From the time I took you under my care I loved you, because I thought that I saw in you a good and benevolent heart. I then wished that your parts might be as good; and they have proved so; they have not only answered my hopes but my most sanguine wishes; I esteem, I admire you, and you are esteemed and admired by others in your now little sphere. But the more I love you now the more I dread the snares and dangers that await you, the next six or seven years of your life, from ill company and bad examples. Should you be corrupted by them what a fall would that be! You would "fall, like setting stars, to rise no more." When you see young fellows, whatever may be their rank, swearing and cursing as senselessly as wickedly, . . . drunk, and engaged in scrapes and quarrels, shun them. *Foenum habent in cornu, longe fuge.* You can only get disgrace and misfortunes by frequenting them. Do not think that these exhorta-

---

[1] In his excellent edition of Chesterfield's Letters to his Godson, the Earl of Carnarvon says : — " This letter, as far as I can decide, is the last of the letters; and Tuesday, June 19, as determined by the chronological tables indicates the year 1770. It is a fitting close to the series."

tions are the formal preachings of a formal old fellow; on the contrary they are the best proofs I can give you of my tenderness. I would have you lead a youth of pleasures; but then for your sake I would have them elegant pleasures becoming a man of sense and a gentleman; they will never sully nor disgrace your character. Keep the best company, both of men and women, and make yourself an interesting figure in it. Have no *mauvaise honte*, which always keeps a man out of good company and sinks him into low and bad company. I really believe that these exhortations and dehortations are unnecessary to your good sense; but however, the danger is so great from the examples of the youth of the present times that I shall frequently return to the charge with my preventives. Mithridates (I think it was) had used himself so much to antidotes that he could not bring it about when he wished to poison himself. What would I not give for such an antidote to administer to you?

. . . .

THE END.

www.ingramcontent.com/pod-product-compliance
Lightning Source LLC
Chambersburg PA
CBHW021957220426
43663CB00007B/855